'Constructive Bloodbath' in Indonesia

'Constructive Bloodbath' in Indonesia

The United States, Britain and the Mass Killings of 1965-66

Nathaniel Mehr

*Foreword by
Carmel Budiardjo*

SPOKESMAN

The author extends his warmest thanks to Dr Robert Cribb of the Australian National University, Canberra, and to Carmel Budiardjo of Tapol, for their advice and assistance at various stages of this project.

© Nathaniel Mehr

Cover design by Tim Coyle

First published in 2009 by
Spokesman Books
Russell House, Bulwell Lane
Nottingham NG6 0BT
England
Phone 0115 970 8318   Fax 0115 9420433
e-mail elfeuro@compuserve.com
www.spokesmanbooks.com

All rights reserved. No part of this publication may be reproduced, stored in a retrieval system or transmitted in any form or by any means, electronic, mechanical, photocopying, recording or otherwise, without the prior permission of the publishers.

ISBN 13 978 085124 767 0

A CIP catalogue is available from the British Library.

Printed by the Russell Press Ltd (phone 0115 978 4505)

Contents

Foreword by Carmel Budiardjo   7

Introduction   13

1. **From Independence to Intrigue**   19
   Indonesia 1950-1965
   Internal Strife, the Rise of the PKI, and the 30th September Movement
   1957-1965
   The Communist Party of Indonesia (PKI)
   The 30th September Movement/ The 'Attempted Coup'

2. **'Pursue, Purge and Destroy'**   40
   The Massacre of the PKI
   The Massacre – Jakarta and Central Java
   East Java
   Bali
   Two Conceptions of Killing: Oriental Madness versus Systemic Massacre

3. **'A Model Destabilisation Plan'**   68
   The United States and Suharto's Rise to Power
   1959-1965: A Change of Policy
   October 1965: The Killing Begins
   Assessing the US Role

4. **'Confrontation' and 'Psychological Warfare'**   94
   Britain and Indonesia in 1965-66
   The Foreign Office and the '30th September Movement'
   1966: Relations Crystallise
   Assessing the British Role

5. **'The Greatest Prize'**   113
   Reflections on the Indonesian Killings
   Suharto's Coup
   Western Journalism and Academic Literature
   The Left
   Conclusion

Bibliography   133

Abbreviations and Acronyms   135

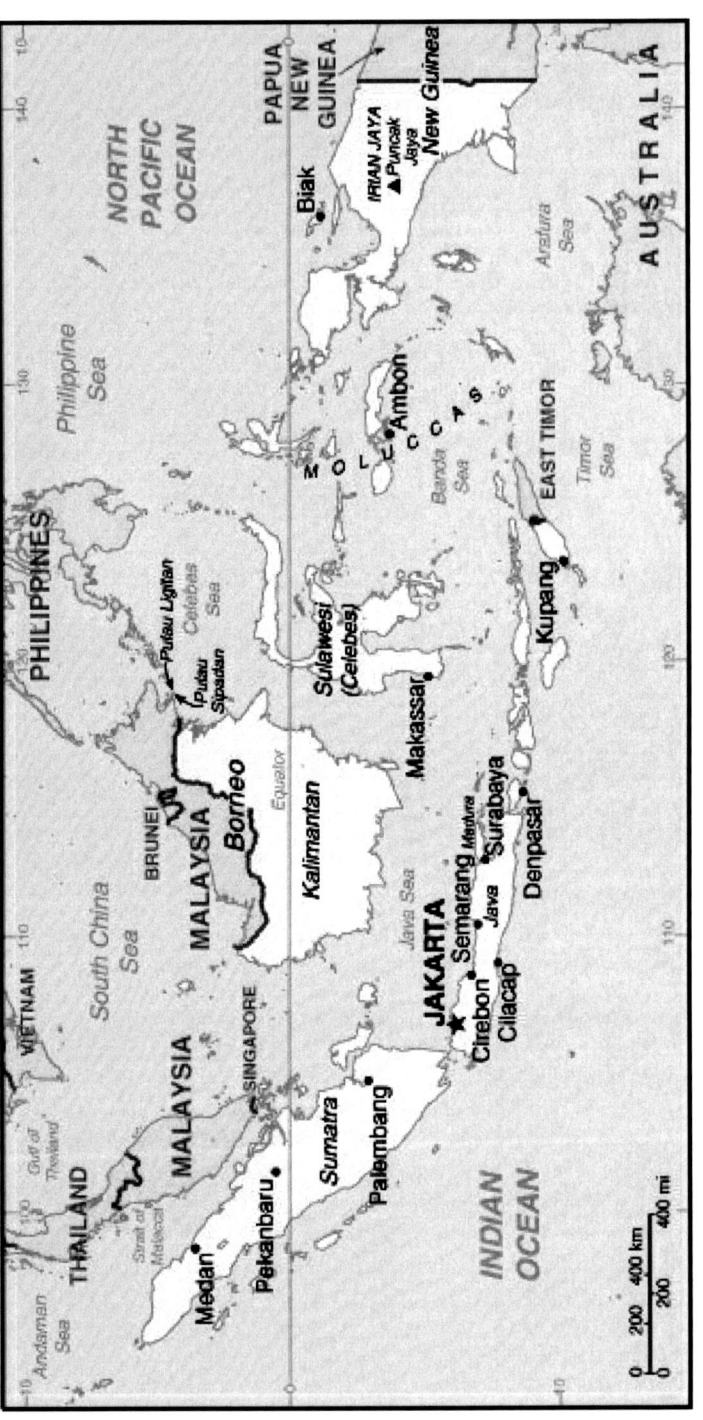

Indonesia

Foreword

Carmel Budiardjo

The terrible events of more than forty years ago, which are meticulously described in this book, still cast a long shadow over Indonesia. Although there has never been any evidence to prove that the Indonesian Communist Party was responsible for the kidnapping and murder of six army generals in 1965, claims about 'attempts to revive communism' frequently result in the abandonment of legitimate activities, for fear of provoking acts of violence.

As I write, one of Indonesia's best-known film-makers, Erros Djarot, has been forced to withdraw his team of actors, actresses and cameramen from Central Java after being banned from filming by the local police because, according to members of the Islamic Defenders' Front, the FPI, his film 'bears the scent of communism'. *Lastri*, a love story set in 1965 in Central Java, is about a woman whose boyfriend suddenly leaves her and goes into hiding. She later marries a young army officer, but the return of her boyfriend four years later confronts her with a terrible dilemma about the decision she made. As Erros Djarot and his 50-person team were forced to pack up and leave, they were wondering whether they would be able to find another location anywhere in Indonesia, without confronting similar obstacles. The weekly magazine, *Tempo*, called this 'censorship by the mob'.

Hearing about this incident reminded me of another one in 2000, also in Central Java. Sulami, a woman I knew well, a former political prisoner like myself, had decided to visit an area where the remains of about twenty victims of the killings in October 1965 lay in unmarked graves. The names of the victims had been carefully recorded by a neighbour, who guided Sulami to the site where many of the bodies had been unceremoniously buried. Her intention was to exhume the remains, identify them one by one with the help of forensic experts, and return them to their families to be given a proper burial. No sooner had she and her friends begun to dig than they were set upon by men brandishing knives, accusing them of 'spreading communism' and threatening their lives. They had no option but to abandon the site, rather than provoke a bloody incident.

Such incidents have occurred with impunity, and without being condemned by the authorities in Jakarta. Such failure to act sets the scene for further threats or acts of violence against those who have tried to heal the wounds of the past.

The only Indonesian President to declare that he would support an investigation into the 1965-66 massacres was Abdurrahman Wahid, the leader of the Muslim organisation, *Nahdlatul Ulama*, many of whose members were responsible for the killings that swept Indonesia in the six months from October 1965. President Wahid said, in April 2000, that it would be 'the government's task to follow the findings of the investigation, to punish those found guilty'. He also said he had 'long ago apologised for the killings of those alleged members of the Communist Party'. His remarks provoked a storm of protest, with one retired general saying that 'people should accept the bloody incident as a part of history'. The man who was then chairman of the country's supreme representative assembly, Amien Rais, from the same party as Wahid, called on the President 'to clarify his apology', adding: 'Indonesia must guard against reviving the communist party and [its] teachings'. A year later, Wahid was impeached for alleged minor financial irregularities and forced to step down.

Earlier this year, it was revealed that Indonesia's National Human Rights Commission, Komnas HAM, a state-funded agency, had since March been investigating violations of human rights following the events of 1965. When asked about the investigations, one member was at first reluctant to confirm the reports, but finally told the press that they were working 'behind the scenes ... in order to avoid stirring up needless controversy'. Such is the atmosphere of suspicion and apprehension surrounding activities of this nature.

After years of silence by those who survived long periods of detention without trial, there has recently been a trickle of information about personal tragedies. One of the most tightly guarded secrets of Suharto's New Order was the infamous banishment of many thousands of men and boys for more than a decade to a remote island, Buru, to fend for themselves in a hazardous environment. The prisoners, all of whom had been classified as 'B category', meaning that they could not be tried 'for lack of sufficient evidence', were forced to clear dense tracts of jungle before they could start planting food and building barracks for themselves. Disease and hunger soon took their toll. Among the prisoners was Pramoedya Ananta Toer, acknowledged as Indonesia's foremost novelist. After his release, in 1979, he published his memoir, *A Mute's Soliloquy* (Nanyian Suni Seorang Bisu), describing their terrible sea journey to Buru aboard a scarcely seaworthy vessel. Many of his fellow prisoners were so lacking in energy because of years of malnourishment that they could barely lift themselves from the floor.

The book includes a list of 325 'Dead and Missing' which Pramoedya had painstakingly compiled from men living in the many units on Buru. The work was never completed because someone leaked news of what he was doing to the authorities. This is the only known record of the fate of prisoners who died on Buru.

Pramoedya was among the first to be arrested in October 1965. One of the worst things he experienced was the destruction of thousands of documents, collected over a period of twenty years, in preparation for an encyclopaedia he was planning to publish. As he was dragged away, pleading for the safe storage of his collection, his library went up in flames. He was struck several times on the head, leaving him deaf in one ear and partially deaf in the other one. A quartet of novels, *The Buru Quartet*, which he authored while on Buru, was not published until many years later, after his release in 1979. Another former prisoner, Jusuf Ishak, founded a publishing house, *Hasta Mitra*, to publish the books, but was continually hounded by the authorities. The quartet, which is part of the school curriculum in neighbouring Malaysia, continued to be banned in Indonesia right up to the time of Pramoedya's death on 30 April 2006.

Two years after Suharto was forced to step down, I was able to visit Indonesia after an absence of nearly thirty years. The most moving of my many encounters was a meeting with more than twenty women, many of whom I knew from my own years of detention. Among them was Sri Ambar, a trade union activist whose terrible sufferings under interrogation had become legendary, even among the prison warders, all of whom were male. There she sat, across the table from me, unable to speak or to hear anything and only able to move with the help of friends. One of her two daughters had been abducted by soldiers, and her mother had been beaten in her presence in an attempt to make her speak. She was one of the few prisoners ever to be tried, and was forced to appear as a witness in the trial of Sudisman, the only top-ranking member of the central committee of the Indonesian Communist Party ever to be tried. She refused to testify, but used her appearance in court to demand the return of her lost daughter.

For many years, former political prisoners were issued with identity cards bearing the letters ET for ex-tapol, which identified them as legitimate targets for discriminatory treatment, such as being barred from public office, being banned from nomination as candidates in elections, and even from voting. They were also denied the right to work as journalists or teachers or in other occupations where they could 'influence the opinions of others'.

All Indonesian citizens over the age of sixty are entitled by law to obtain a lifetime ID without discrimination. But many have been denied this right. The latest example is 67-year old Nani Nurani, who fought for six years to claim this right. Efforts on her behalf by the Jakarta Legal Aid Foundation proved fruitless, so she took her complaint to the local court. The court's decision in her favour was reversed on appeal, and it was finally the Supreme Court that ruled in her favour in October 2008. There are without doubt many former prisoners who have experienced the same humiliation but prefer to let the matter rest, rather that draw attention to themselves and their families. The ET stigma, which has now been removed from identity cards, still blights the lives of many who were held for years without ever being found guilty in a court of law. Whatever the law prescribes, interpretation is left to local officials; with the anti-communist mindset still being so pervasive, countless former prisoners still suffer such indignities.

Nani was among the many teenagers whom I met when I was incarcerated in Bukit Duri Prison, from 1969 till 1971: young women, some as young as thirteen when they were arrested, who had fallen foul of the regime for getting involved in youthful gatherings of no political significance whatever, yet which resulted in their incarceration for many years. We, the older inmates, called them 'the children', to whom I devoted a chapter in my book, *Surviving Indonesia's Gulag*.

Nani's lawyer, Asfinawati, head of the Legal Aid Foundation, said: 'Society still sees them as people who should be ostracised. They fear the consequences of getting close to former political prisoners. The New Order regime made sure it worked that way ... They made sure the stigma stuck.'

Suharto, the man who ruled Indonesia with a rod of iron for thirty-two years, was never brought to justice. As he lay dying in January 2008, tributes were paid at his bedside by present and former presidents of Indonesia, and many of the country's foremost personalities. Attempts to bring him to justice, for the greed and corruption that earned him notoriety as one of the world's richest men, foundered on claims that he was too ill to appear in court. But his multiple crimes against humanity in Indonesia, the systematic massacre of hundreds of thousands of people in 1965-1966, and the brutalities inflicted on the people of East Timor during the twenty-four years of their country's occupation, were never subject to any legal challenge. Among the many Indonesian generals who have been allowed to enjoy impunity for the part they played in the 'Constructive Bloodbath' described in the following pages, Suharto is the most criminal of them all.

London, December 2008

As two men await certain death, a soldier bayonets those at his feet. (October 1965)

Introduction

On 27th January 2008, Indonesia's former president Suharto died peacefully in his sleep, aged eighty-six. Suharto was the central figure in the authoritarian government which had ruled Indonesia with an iron fist from 1967 to 1998. His regime is credited with having effected Indonesia's wholesale integration into the world capitalist economy, bringing to an abrupt end the tentative and somewhat ambivalent flirtation with socialism embarked upon by his predecessor Sukarno. Suharto's meteoric rise – from an apparently uncontroversial and apolitical Major General in the Indonesian army to the undisputed presidency of the entire country in a matter of weeks – was facilitated by a quite remarkable set of events played out over a six-month period from October 1965 to April 1966. At the centre of these events was a systematic massacre of hundreds of thousands of innocent people, whose sole crime was their affiliation – actual, suspected or alleged – with the Indonesian Communist Party (PKI). Prior to October 1965, the PKI had been a major player in Indonesian national politics, their success founded on a strong support base among Indonesia's rural poor. The killings left the PKI completely decimated, ending the party's participation in Indonesian politics and clearing the way for the seizure of state power by a small military clique headed by Suharto. With conservative estimates reckoning a death toll of approximately 500,000, the killings constitute one of the most devastating mass murders of modern times, yet relatively little is known about them in the West. This is somewhat surprising, given the level of attention that ordinarily accrues, both in the education system and in the media discourse, to brutal, large-scale atrocities such as this one. The majority of people in the West will have learnt, at school, about the atrocities committed by Adolf Hitler's Nazi regime during the Second World War; with regard to the post-war period, most people in the West have at least heard or read something about the appalling massacres carried out by the pseudo-communist Khmer Rouge regime of Pol Pot in Cambodia in the 1970s. By contrast, relatively few people have heard anything about the Indonesian killings of 1965-66, although a chapter in John Pilger's 2003 book *The New Rulers of the World* did help to bring the subject to the attention of a wider audience.

The purpose of this study is to provide a detailed narrative of these events, and consider the power politics, internal and global, which brought about such a massive slaughter of innocent lives. Along the way, a number of prevalent assumptions will be examined and questioned. Many existing accounts of the Indonesian massacres put forward a narrative of events along the following lines: the PKI attempted to overthrow the Indonesian government in a coup attempt on 30th September 1965; the coup attempt failed, leading to a retributive purge of leading PKI members carried out by the Indonesian army under the leadership of Suharto, who would replace Sukarno as President a year and a half later; the purge got out of hand in some areas, leading to unintended mass deaths, on account of over-zealousness on the part of young extremists. As this study will show, this simplistic interpretation is unsatisfactory and misleading in a number of important respects. There is some doubt as to whether the so-called 'coup attempt' was really a 'coup attempt' in the proper sense, given that it appears to have been conceived as a pre-emptive mutiny by middle-ranking officers seeking to preserve the status quo, rather than overthrow the government and seize state power; much of the available evidence suggests that it is by no means certain that the PKI was the instigator of the mutiny of 30th September 1965, as the Suharto regime subsequently claimed; the PKI purge was not merely targeted at the senior PKI leadership – it was a systematic, army-organised attempt to kill as many PKI members, irrespective of seniority, as conveniently possible. Finally, the mass killing facilitated the rise to power of Suharto who, though only formally inaugurated some eighteen months later, achieved effective power as early as April 1966, laying the foundations for a dictatorship that would last for thirty-two years. While the historiography has tended to focus on the one 'coup' that was unsuccessful, this study will identify Suharto's grab for power, from October 1965 to April 1966, as meeting received definitions of a 'coup' rather more accurately than the rebellion of 30th September 1965. Each of these themes will be explored in detail. In addition, I shall examine the role played by the United States and Great Britain in supporting Suharto's military takeover of Indonesia.

Chapter One provides a brief summary of the development of

Indonesian political history from 1950 to October 1965. During this period, the newly-independent state went through numerous changes of government alongside severe economic problems. The internal political background to the 'coup' of 30th September 1965 is examined in some depth, as this was the event which triggered the mass killing of communists and alleged communists which began in October. A detailed account of the killings themselves, featuring eyewitness evidence, comprises Chapter Two. I make no apology for the graphic and gruesome nature of some of the accounts in this second chapter – the sheer savagery of the butchery would be obscured by a narrative restricted to cold statistics. In particular, the sadistic brutality of the young men from Indonesia's various Muslim youth organisations, who carried out many of the killings with the express blessing of senior Muslim figures in Indonesia, deserves highlighting as evidence of the most vile hypocrisy on the part of individuals and organisations purporting to represent a pious and god-fearing worldview. The role of the US government in nurturing and supporting the Suharto clique, as well as providing support for the Generals during and after the killings, forms the focus of Chapter Three. For the United States, the events of 1965-66 were the culmination of a policy embarked upon at the end of the 1950s, whereby the US cultivated a strong relationship with senior sections of the Indonesian military in order to militate against the possibility that the PKI might some day turn its growing popular support into real, effective political power. The elimination of the PKI was hailed in unqualified terms as a triumph by US policymakers, who expressed little or no concern for the human rights of the hundreds of thousands of people who lost their lives in the process. The US stance is echoed in the position of Great Britain, whose rather more limited role in the events of 1965-66 forms the subject of Chapter Four. Britain was technically at war with Indonesia – engaged in a 'low intensity conflict' in the forests of Malaysia – when the killing started in October 1965. Like the Americans, the British took the view that any amount of barbarism would be justified for the ultimate end of preventing Indonesia from succumbing to the scourge of communism. In the wake of the 'coup attempt' of 30th September 1965, Britain assisted in the destabilisation of Indonesia by spreading anti-communist propaganda which served to encourage violence against the PKI. A concluding fifth chapter looks at the long-term consequences for Indonesia of Suharto's rise to power, and reflects on how the killings have been treated in the West, drawing from the academic historiography and media commentary.

Indonesia's place within the Cold War battlefield tends to frame much of the historiography on the killings, and also offers the most plausible explanation for the striking failure of political and media institutions in the United States and Great Britain to issue, with respect to the killings, the sort of outraged moral condemnation quite rightly heaped upon the likes of Pol Pot and Stalin. While the violence of the Cambodian killing fields and the Stalinist purges was perpetrated by regimes professing an affiliation with socialism, the killings in Indonesia were organised by avowedly anti-communist Generals who sought to integrate that country into the global capitalist system, with the aim of turning Indonesia into an anti-communist stronghold in the region. As we shall see, Western reaction has, in the main, ranged from denial and distortion at one extreme, to solemn stoicism about the perceived necessity of the slaughter at the other. At the political level, Suharto would be rewarded with decades of American and British patronage, in the form of military and economic aid and political support. It is in view of this discrepancy that I have borrowed, for the title of this work, the term 'constructive bloodbath' from Noam Chomsky and Edward Herman's *The Washington Connection and Third World Fascism*, in which the authors use the term to connote those instances in which physical violence that would ordinarily incur the strongest moral condemnation is endorsed at state level, and variously distorted, played down, or denied outright at media level, on account of the fact that the violence in question has resulted in an outcome beneficial to the United States' strategic and/or economic policy in the context of the struggle for global supremacy in the Cold War period. The killings of 1965-66 did not merely help to keep the immense natural resources of the Indonesian archipelago within the American sphere of influence – Suharto's accession to power precipitated the opening up of the country to exploitation by foreign capital in a manner unprecedented in its scale and brazen cynicism, so the position of international (largely US) corporate interests in the region was not merely protected but actually considerably enhanced. The political orientation of the Suharto clique offers the most persuasive explanation for the morally indefensible position adopted by the American and British governments with respect to the new regime and its murderous baptism: the massacre of half a million innocent people in Indonesia served to destroy the PKI as an effective political force, and was therefore, in Cold War terms, 'constructive'.

If the centrality of Cold War strategy is essential to any serious attempt to understand the Western involvement in Indonesia since World War Two, the logic of Cold War necessity has also underpinned the substantial apologist discourse in relation to the killings. At the heart of the issue lies a semantic anomaly which informed the very essence of the political culture of international relations in the capitalist world during the 1948-1991 period. The very notion that the struggle of US-led global capitalism against all forms of socialism and communism constituted a 'war' was an ingenious deception that provided a self-serving justification for violence – however civilised a society may be, in a war situation, it may unhesitatingly avail itself of the right to carry out exceptional violence in self-defence, without incurring moral censure: this is a principle with which few people, irrespective of political persuasion, would seriously disagree. The presentation of the struggle for global supremacy as an essentially defensive struggle for survival served to alter the moral framework in which Western foreign policy officials operated during the period in question. It was, of course, premised upon a falsehood – a PKI-dominated Indonesia would, in all probability, have posed no threat to the United States, in military terms; just as it is inconceivable that Salvador Allende's socialist government in Chile in 1973 (which was overthrown by a US-sponsored military coup) represented any serious military threat to the US or her allies. The ideological struggle against communism was therefore a struggle, not for survival, but for global economic supremacy, couched in the language of 'security'. However, the struggle took on an apocalyptic aspect, which was exploited to the maximum by the political establishments in both the United States and Great Britain, and internalised uncritically in much of the academic and media discourse in those countries. As a consequence, a significant school of opinion remains convinced that the Indonesian killings of 1965-66 represented a regrettable necessity in an era in which the struggle against global communism was perceived as a matter of life and death, and moral certainties were accordingly blurred or suspended.

Almost two decades after the end of the Cold War, and with the greater objectivity conferred by a distance of time, this study presents a concise narrative of these events, providing a sober re-assessment untainted by Cold War ideological chauvinism. The killings are not simply considered in isolation – they formed the most dramatic and shocking stage of a long-term shift in Indonesia that would see the country subjected to one of the world's most detested dictatorships. Nevertheless, given the horror and the sheer scale of the slaughter, it is only appropriate that the killings should form the central focus of this study. Of course, questions of moral judgment ought, properly, to be left to the reader. Nevertheless the cold, murderous cynicism exhibited by the primary perpetrators of the massacre – the Indonesian army – as well as by their patrons in the West, leaves little scope for exculpation, and only the most fervent right-wing ideologue would deny that the politically-motivated mass killings of 1965-66 constitute a criminal atrocity, a tragic episode in Indonesian and world history, and a shameful blot on the reputations of the United States and Great Britain, the two chief co-sponsors of the Suharto regime.

CHAPTER ONE

From Independence to Intrigue

Indonesia 1950-1965

*Internal Strife, the Rise of the PKI,
and the 30th September Movement*

By the time the new nation of Indonesia proclaimed its independence in August 1945, the population of the archipelago – encompassing over fourteen thousand islands, most prominent amongst which were the islands of Java, Sumatra, Borneo and Celebes – had fought two long and bloody wars of liberation, first against the Dutch, whose colonial interests had controlled the archipelago for in excess of some three hundred years, and then the Japanese, who invaded the country in 1942 and occupied it until their defeat in the Second World War. Sukarno[1], the charismatic and hugely popular nationalist who had led the country to freedom and independence, became the country's first President. From the very moment of its birth, the Indonesian nation would have to fight for its survival. Dutch efforts to re-assert their supremacy triggered a bitter revolutionary war of independence (1945-49) from which the new Indonesian nation, with Sukarno at its head, emerged victorious. From 1950 until the end of his effective rule in 1966, the chief aim of Sukarno's presidency would be to preserve the fragile unity of a nation which was as fragmented politically and socially as it was geographically. In order to understand the events of 1965-66, it is necessary to review the preceding decade-and-a-half of domestic politics which gave rise to the atmosphere of intrigue and uncertainty which precipitated the crisis. Broadly speaking, Indonesia political life in this period may be split into two distinct phases, the first comprising an attempt at a representative parliamentary system (1950-57), and the second characterised by an anti-democratic and autocratic approach, euphemistically entitled 'Guided Democracy' (1957-65).[2]

1950-57

The 1950-57 period was one of qualified progress for the Indonesian nation, alongside significant demographic and social change. Huge swathes of the rural population left subsistence farming for the wage labour of the cities – the population of the capital, Jakarta, doubled to 1.8 million between 1945 and 1955, and had grown further to 2.9 million by 1961. The Indonesian language was firmly established as the national language, a significant development in a nation whose disparate elements boasted some four hundred languages in total, complemented by a steep rise in adult literacy and an increase in newspaper circulation between 1950 and 1956, from 500,000 to 933,000. Whilst the Indonesian nation could therefore claim to be achieving some degree of cultural and intellectual self-sufficiency as a natural progression from, and manifestation of, its political independence, there was little doubt that the Indonesian nation was not independent economically. Foreign companies maintained a significant presence in the country – Shell, Stanvac and Caltext were strong in the oil industry, inter-island shipping was controlled by the Dutch KPM line, and banking was dominated by Dutch, British and Chinese interests.

Domestic politics were dominated by four political parties during this period. Masyumi, which represented Islamic political interests, was the largest political party in Indonesia in the early 1950s. It had adopted a pragmatic tactic of avoiding doctrinaire positions that could potentially associate it with separatist or Islamic revolutionary ambitions and incur the hostility of the fervently nationalistic central government, for whom national unity, and the preservation of the existing system of government, were utterly paramount. The second largest party was the Indonesian Nationalist Party (PNI), whose support base consisted mainly of white-collar workers and bureaucrats, along with the *abangan* (nominal) Muslims[3]. The PNI was the party most closely associated with Sukarno, and was viewed by modernisers as an important check against the aspirations of political Islam in Indonesia. The Indonesian Socialist Party (PSI) had support among Jakarta intellectuals and higher civil servants, but little popular support outside these circles. The Indonesian Communist Party (PKI) found its support base among urban and agricultural estate workers, who were organised through the PKI-affiliated trade union federation SOBSI. The PKI adopted a policy of co-operation with non-communist forces, which it justified on pragmatic grounds (see below). Apart from these four parties, only the Christian parties (Catholic and Protestant) and the Partai Murba (Proletarian Party) carried any influence.

Although Indonesia's nationalists had proclaimed that theirs was a 'national revolution', the exact political identity of the 'revolutionary' aspect of the struggle was far from clear. Sukarno himself was not a communist, but his recognition of the important role played by Marxists and communists in the national liberation struggles of the 1940s manifested itself in a broadly sympathetic approach towards Indonesia's communists, and respect for the communists' right to participate in Indonesian political life. Sukarno's political approach was informed above all else by a belief that only compromise would save the fragile new nation from fragmentation and a premature death. The Indonesian state philosophy would therefore be centred on a set of broad principles (*Pancasila* – the 'five principles': belief in God, humanity, national unity, democracy and social justice) in a move carefully designed to draw in nationalists, socialists and Muslims under the umbrella of an all-encompassing, inclusive national ideology. With memories of the independence struggle still fresh, the need to prioritise national unity above political or religious factionalism was broadly accepted within the Indonesian body politic during the 1950s, and so the period was characterised by a series of coalitions, with socialist parties forming improbable alliances with Islamic groups, who in turn fostered relationships with modernising secular nationalists. The first of these alliances was the Masyumi-PNI coalition which lasted for seven months from September 1950, enjoying favourable economic circumstances brought about by a commodity boom resulting from the outbreak of the Korean War. A Masyumi-PNI coalition replaced it in April 1951, and implemented a police crackdown on the PKI after a series of strikes. When a second Masyumi-PNI coalition passed a bill in April 1953 scheduling parliamentary elections for 1955, the country's politicians set about trying to build mass support. The PKI made impressive gains during this period, claiming a party membership of one million by the end of

1955, up from 165,206 in March 1954; the party's affiliated peasant organisation, the BTI, had a membership of 3.3million (up from 360,000 in September 1953). Ninety-five per cent of registered voters turned out to vote in the parliamentary elections. As expected, the PNI and Masyumi came out on top, winning respectively 22.3% and 20.9% of the vote (the Muslim vote was split between Masyumi and a rival Muslim party, Nahdlatul Ulama [NU]. NU won 18.4% of the vote). The strong showing of the PKI, who came fourth with 16.4% of the vote, came as a particular shock to the PNI, who now identified the PKI as a singular threat to the PNI's position as the country's prominent non-religious party. After an unsatisfactory coalition between the PNI, Masyumi and NU collapsed in March 1956, a new parliament was assembled on 26th March 1965. This would be the first parliament in Indonesia's history to be elected by a free choice by universal adult suffrage – and the last until 1999.

The Indonesian army, which had played a prominent role in the armed struggles of the 1940s, continued to wield considerable influence in the political life of the independent Indonesian state. A breakdown in the balance of power within the military would ultimately lead to the end of the country's brief experiment with parliamentary democracy. In November 1955, the army's new chief of staff, General Abdul Haris Nasution, announced plans for a large-scale transfer of officers. Nasution's proposed reforms were in direct conflict with the interests of many army officers, who were firmly entrenched in private business agreements contingent upon maintaining the status quo. Upon its implementation in 1956, the programme caused a major split in the army, with pro-Sukarno, pro-PNI officers on one side, and a pro-Masyumi faction, supported by non-Javanese officers hostile to the central government in Jakarta, on the other. The tensions culminated in a botched coup attempt which was defeated by Nasution. Nasution used the opportunity to consolidate his personal position, arresting or transferring his opponents. A new crisis emerged in December 1956, when disaffected army officers in Sumatra – many of them veterans of the revolutionary period – rebelled against Jakarta with significant civilian support. Although this was not a separatist movement, it looked to the central government in Jakarta as though Sumatra,

Indonesia's richest island, was on the verge of breaking away and forming an autonomous unit, and the crisis deepened in early 1957 as similar rebellions occurred in Bali and Sulawesi and Maluku (this became known as the 'Permesta rebellion' – from *Per*juangan Se*mest*a *A*lam – meaning 'universal struggle'). With the Indonesian state apparently disintegrating before his eyes a mere twelve years after declaring independence, Sukarno effectively ended parliamentary democracy in Indonesia by proclaiming martial law in March 1957, succumbing to pressure from the nationalist and Islamic parties to halt the rise of the PKI, who had been making steady gains under the electoral system (see 'The PKI', below).

1957-1965

'Guided Democracy' was the label used by Sukarno to explain the system of government put in place in 1957 to keep the Indonesian nation together. In May 1957, a National Council was created, consisting of forty-one representatives from 'functional groups', and some *ex officio* members. Although there was to be no direct representation, most political parties found indirect representation through their affiliations to 'functional groups'. Masyumi and the Catholic Party were, however, expressly excluded, on the grounds of their association with the Permesta rebellion. In June 1957, General Nasution began establishing army-civilian cooperation bodies to detach the 'functional groups' from the political parties; at the same time, PSI and PKI politicians were targeted in a campaign of arrests aimed, ostensibly, at stamping out corruption. Although Sukarno did not quite exercise the sort of personal dictatorship of a pre-colonial Javanese king, 'Guided Democracy' meant, in practice, a return to the sort of repressive state apparatus of Dutch and Japanese colonial domination. This was broadly in line with Nasution's own ideological outlook; he was pushing for a corporatist, military state in which political parties would be abolished and the public sphere rendered entirely devoid of any hint of political pluralism. The veteran politician Sjahrir warned in 1958 that Nasution's vision constituted 'a militaristic and fascist ideal'.[4]

During this period, Sukarno and the PKI developed a relationship based upon mutual convenience. The PKI, under constant threat from the army and the more zealous Islamic elements, needed Sukarno's protection in order to get ahead politically; Sukarno, for his part, hoped be able to use the PKI's effective grass-roots political organisation to mobilise the masses in his favour, to check the growing power of the Indonesian army. Provincial council elections in July and August 1957 confirmed the PKI's growing popularity. The party won 34% of the vote in Central and East Java, came second in East Java by only 3% to NU, also displacing the PNI in second place in West Java. In the meantime, it became increasingly clear that the activities of the various movements for regional autonomy would not abate, despite the best efforts of 'Guided Democracy'. An unsuccessful attempt on Sukarno's life in November 1957 by Islamic zealots offered a hint of what was to come[5], and in February the Indonesian government faced another outright rebellion. The PRRI rebels, led by Sjafruddin Prawiranegara, announced a rebel government in Sumatra in February, and were soon joined, in Sulawesi, by veterans of the Permesta campaign. The rebels received the backing of the Masyumi party, as well as covert support from the United States government. The rebellion would be crushed by the army in a long struggle lasting until January 1962, and Nasution immediately seized the opportunity to purge the army of dissident officers and personal opponents, leaving himself as the undisputed leader of the army. The rebellion fractured Indonesia's relations with the United States, and discredited Masyumi and the PSI. Both parties were formally banned in August 1960. In July 1959, Sukarno dissolved the Constituent Assembly, and he later replaced the National Council with a new Supreme Advisory Council and a National Planning Council. The net effect of the changes was an increasing tendency for power and influence to be contingent upon personal access to Sukarno and a small number of leading Generals, rather than through institutions. An August 1959 makeover (a new acronym, Manipol, meaning *Manifesto Politik* – 'Political Manifesto' would enter the Sukarno lexicon) could not hide the drift towards an autocratic and secretive style of government under 'Guided Democracy'.

By contrast with the declining fortunes of the PSI and Masyumi, the PKI was believed to be represented by between 17% and 25% of the appointees who made up the so-called 'mutual co-operation' parliament in August 1960, and the party was represented in every government institution except the cabinet. The army's position was also growing stronger by the day – the army's tentative move into the lucrative oil industry, via a new state-run oil company, Permina, which would oversee the nationalisation of Dutch-run businesses, was particularly significant. While a series of unsuccessful deflationary steps exacerbated the country's economic problems in the early 1960s – inflation would reach around 100% per year in the period 1961 to 1964 – the army's internal strength would be reinforced in 1961 by a £450million arms loan from the Soviet Union. Fearing another Permesta or PRRI-style rebellion, Sukarno produced an updated, re-branded version of the *Pancasila* doctrine for the 1960s. A new acronym – *Nasakom* – would entail a vision of a united Indonesia based upon *Nationalisme, Agama,* and *Komunisme*: nationalism, Islam, and Marxism. This was a clear attempt to incorporate supporters of PNI, Masyumi/NU and the PKI into a shared vision for the Indonesian nation. However, the inclusive rhetoric of *Nasakom* was at odds with the impoverishing effects of major reforms implemented in 1963 at the behest of the International Monetary Fund, which made financial assistance conditional upon far-reaching budgetary changes. State budgets were cut and credit was tightened in May 1963, and the currency was again devalued; government salaries, by contrast, were doubled. The reforms were greeted with a storm of public protest, especially from small businessmen, who stood to lose out heavily from the austerity measures.

Events in the international sphere took centre-stage in September 1963, when Sukarno reacted angrily to the Malaysian declaration of independence. Sukarno took the view that the new federation amounted to a British neo-colonial stronghold right on Indonesia's doorstep. In view of the fact that the PRRI rebellion had drawn support from Malayan and Singaporean circles, Sukarno viewed this new development as posing a direct threat to Indonesian national security, and immediately severed all relations with Malaya and Singapore. This policy, which drew active support from the PKI, would culminate in the 'Confrontation' with Britain (see Chapter Four), and served as a useful distraction from the country's mounting domestic economic and political problems (inflation reached 134% in

1964). The expansion of the conflict into the Malay Peninsula in May 1964 was a concern to the anti-communist army leadership. They had initially acquiesced in the venture with the hope of obtaining political benefits for the army – in fact, the army leadership was now increasingly being by-passed by Sukarno's decision-making process. By contrast, the PKI's confidence grew in proportion with its political influence (see 'The PKI', below), and the army, in turn, came to identify the party as a direct threat to their continued hegemony. In 1964, right-wing elements within the army began to cultivate links with the proscribed NU and other Islamic groups, with a view to checking the progress of the party. Sukarno's endorsement, in January 1965, of the PKI's proposal to arm the workers and peasants to create a 'Fifth Force' in the national security apparatus (to supplement the existing four: the army, navy, air force and police), did little to assuage the Generals' fears. The appointment of 'Nasakom advisers', drawn from PKI ranks, to assist existing armed forces units, provided further cause for concern. Meanwhile, in the international sphere, Jakarta's alliance with the communist People's Republic of China, apparently sealed by Sukarno's decision to withdraw Indonesia from the UN in protest at Malaysia's admission to the Security Council, indirectly conferred special prestige upon the PKI by endorsing, as a matter of state policy, a Marxist or quasi-Marxist anti-imperialist stance.

A number of developments in 1965 intensified the sense of polarisation in Indonesian politics. In response to Sukarno's decision to ban twenty-one newspapers with anti-PKI leanings, in February, the army began to publish its own newspapers. That same month, the army took over the management of a handful of US business enterprises which had been seized by PKI unions; the Stanvac, Caltex and Shell companies were now under army-run state supervision. Despite the reluctance of senior Generals to accept Sukarno's 'Fifth Force' proposal of arming the peasantry, Sukarno endorsed an Air Force programme giving short training courses to civilians from the PKI's mass organisations at the Air Force base at Halim, in an operation that appeared, to the Generals, to be uncomfortably close to the spirit of the 'Fifth Force' proposal. By September 1965, some two thousand civilians had attended these courses. After discussions with Sukarno, the army explicitly rejected both the 'Fifth Force' proposal and the President's appeal for what he called the 'Nasakomisation' of the army, a nebulous concept which entailed greater integration of PKI officials within the upper strata of the Indonesian army. Military suspicions were further raised when the Air Force chief Omar Dhani embarked upon a secret trip to China to discuss a Chinese offer to provide a small arms shipment; the country's most senior army figure, General Nasution, was neither consulted nor given prior notification of the visit, fuelling suspicions that the arms shipment was intended for the purposes of arming the peasantry in defiance of the military's express rejection of that proposal. The suspicion was, however, mutual. Throughout September 1965, rumours abounded that senior Generals, led by General Nasution and General Yani, were planning a coup against Sukarno, to take place on the nation's Armed Forces Day on 5th October, with the aim of seizing control of the state and checking the rise of the PKI. In the event, things moved rather faster than that.

The Communist Party of Indonesia (PKI)

Founded in 1914, the PKI started life as the Indies Social Democratic Association (ISDV) under Dutch colonial rule, changing its name to the Partai Komunis Indonesia in 1920, inspired by the communist October Revolution in Russia in 1917. After a series of revolts in the late 1920s, the party was driven underground by the Dutch authorities, leading to the execution and imprisonment of a number of its leaders. The PKI would remain an underground organisation for the remainder of Dutch colonial rule, only emerging as a force in Indonesian politics after the Revolution of 1945-49.[6] During the revolution, the PKI staged an armed uprising against Sukarno in the town of Madiun in East Java in 1948. The uprising was defeated, and the PKI was widely denounced among Indonesian nationalists across the political spectrum for having betrayed the cause of Indonesian nationalism by staging an internal rebellion at the very time when unity against the common Dutch enemy was seen as imperative.

When Dipa Nusantara Aidit took over the leadership of the party, in 1951, the PKI moved away from the underground approach preferred by many party stalwarts, adopting instead a policy of cooperation with other, non-communist parties. The new leadership gave some consideration to the adoption a policy of armed struggle.[7] This was ultimately rejected in favour of a non-violent strategy; the leadership cited the nation's unusual geographic and demographic composition – the impracticability of guerrilla warfare across the disparate islands of the archipelago, together with the densely populated nature of the islands' towns and cities, made armed struggle unworkable. Instead, Aidit believed that the party should be active among the Indonesian masses in order to build a broad united front in its pursuit of political power, rather than confining itself to the narrower aim of achieving parliamentary success.[8] Aidit sought to shift the emphasis away from intellectual theorising, in favour of a more practical emphasis on achieving support at the grass-roots of Indonesian society: 'The people do not want Marxist-Leninist theses. The want, instead, improvement in their lot.'[9] In a significant revision of orthodox Marxist views on class struggle, Aidit asserted that the Indonesian proletariat ought to 'build unity with the national bourgeoisie and preserve this unity with all its strength.' He cited Indonesia's status as a newly-independent nation under threat from neo-colonialist forces – Indonesia's bourgeoisie was itself 'being oppressed by foreign imperialism', and could therefore 'under certain circumstances and within certain limits, participate in the struggle against imperialism'[10]. This was a significant departure from the orthodox Marxist perspective, which viewed the proletariat-bourgeoisie division as something that transcended national boundaries and was fundamentally irreconcilable. This controversial position would form the basis of the PKI's policy under Aidit. Aidit set out the core of his thinking in *The Road to People's Democracy for Indonesia* (1954): the alliance with the bourgeoisie would be founded on, and mirrored by, 'the firm unity between the workers and the peasants, the largest and most oppressed group of the Indonesian people'.[11] He welcomed the exclusion of the Masyumi and PSI, in 1953, as a return to a 'united anti-imperialist national front'. Aidit refused to contemplate any suggestion that his united front policy constituted a compromise of Marxist principles; rather, he believed he was adapting a Marxist-Leninist ideology to the peculiarities of the Indonesian situation.[12]

Aidit's approach drew him into an open ideological conflict with the USSR, which was during this period pursuing a pragmatic policy of supporting non-communist governments in the underdeveloped world, provided they were prepared to break ties with the West and establish new bonds with the socialist states. The Chinese took the view that this policy, which tended to manifest itself in Russian support for bourgeois and anti-communist regimes, constituted a sell-out of national liberation movements and socialist movements in the underdeveloped world. Aidit agreed with this view, and in 1963 even went so far as to question whether the Moscow government could rightly call itself socialist: 'A socialist country cannot be counted as one if it does not come to the aid of the struggle for independence'.[13] In response to charges that Aidit's own policy of co-operation with Sukarno's bourgeois state constituted an anachronism in the context of orthodox Marxist thinking, Aidit claimed that the 'progressive aspect' of the state had, under Sukarno, become its 'main aspect', superseding the state's repressive and reactionary nature.[14] The PKI's split with the Soviet Union was confirmed when Aidit declined an invitation to a convention of the world's communist parties in Moscow scheduled for 1st March 1965. For its part, the USSR would continue to provide military funding and equipment for the Indonesian army, right through the crisis and mass killings of 1965-66.

Within a few years of his accession to the leadership of the party, Aidit had overseen a remarkable resurgence in the party's fortunes. Having been almost completely eradicated in the purges after the Madiun affair of 1948, and having been the target of repression under the Masyumi-PNI coalition in the early 1950s, the party emerged to poll 16.4% of the vote in the 1955 elections. Having resolved to establish a popular support base among the peasantry, who comprised some 70% of the population of Indonesia, the PKI championed the cause of land reform in rural areas. Aidit targeted a number of foreign-owned plantations, especially in Sumatra, describing the system of land tenure as '100% feudalism'.[15] This was tempered by the promise of a degree of protection for the land rights of those among the rich and middling peasants who were prepared to ally themselves with the PKI.[16] In the late 1950s, the PKI implemented a policy aimed at increasing the party's presence in the villages in order to facilitate moves towards reform; this policy (the 'Go Down' movement) involved sending party cadres 'down' into the villages to live, eat and work with the peasants.[17]

In 1959-60, the party achieved their most significant success at the legislative level, with the passing of two land reform bills with potentially far-reaching effects. The Crop Sharing Law, passed in November 1959, provided for a minimum 50-50 splitting of crops between landlords and tenants, along with other provisions improving the position of tenants.[18] The Basic Agrarian Law, passed in September 1960, aimed at a fundamental overhaul of Indonesia's outdated land ownership system, with the aim of providing greater security for agricultural workers and a stronger position for Indonesian farmers vis-à-vis foreign plantation owners; the law provided for a minimum entitlement of two hectares of land per family, and included provisions penalising absentee landlords. The effective implementation of the reforms was impeded to a certain extent by inefficient administrative practices, but to a far greater extent by a deliberate policy, on the part of many landlords, of simply ignoring the new legal requirements, or else deliberately obstructing their implementation by carrying out the illegal transfer of lands to relatives and 'dummy' buyers.[19] Although the land reform policy had now passed into national law, the landlords, confident that they had strong support in the influential PNI and military circles, were intent on treating the law as an aberration that did not need to be taken seriously. The landlords even had sympathetic friends among the very committees established in order to oversee and direct the implementation of the reform.[20] The land reform laws set the PKI on a collision course with the landlords. A vigorous campaign for full implementation of the laws, on the part of various peasant organisations affiliated with the PKI and joined by sympathetic left-wing groups, faced determined opposition from the PNI, Islamic groups and the military, culminating in violent confrontations in 1965. In the meantime, concerns were being raised as to whether the party had sacrificed discipline and organisation in its apparently successful bid to obtain a mass following; in July 1965, the party's Secretary General Sudisman noted an apparent increase in factional and disciplinary problems.[21] By contrast, the army was becoming increasingly sophisticated in its approach to winning back the popular support it had been losing to the PKI, setting up its own civilian front organisations to rival the PKI's affiliated peasant and trade union groups (BTI and SOBSI) whilst continuing with localised suppression of the PKI.[22]

The PKI had made tremendous progress during the 1950-65 period. However, the party did not occupy any official positions of note in the various cabinets of the 1950-57 period, and thereafter its improved standing was contingent upon Sukarno's support in the face of continued opposition from the military. Under 'Guided Democracy', the fundamental policy differences between the army and the PKI became increasingly apparent, crystallising into a position of unqualified mutual antagonism by 1965. This was a power struggle conducted in an essentially nationalistic framework, as the PKI and the army vied for primacy in the hotly-contested national mythology of the young Indonesian state. The PKI saw themselves as the true heirs to the Indonesian national revolution of 1945-49, arguing that the army's role was only related to the primary stages of that revolution, namely the expulsion of foreign occupying forces. They conceived of the Indonesian revolution as an ongoing and dynamic phenomenon, in which the next stage would be to hand greater political and administrative responsibility to the people; the PKI's favoured policies – military training for the civilian population, greater civilian involvement in governmental administration, and a more prominent role for trade unions – would constitute the next stages in the revolution.[23] The army, by contrast, saw both independence and the prominence of the military in the political and economic life of the country as ends in themselves. Entrenched in a position of privilege achieved and consolidated over the 1950-65 period, the army correctly perceived the PKI's reform programme as a direct attack upon its privileges.

Sukarno's ruthless suppression of the PKI uprising at Madiun in 1948 cemented his reputation as a fervent anti-communist. However, the 1957 elections had shown the PKI to be the second largest party in Indonesia, and Sukarno took the view that the most effective way to neutralise the party would be to co-opt it, allowing the PKI a significant degree of legitimacy and influence, within an overall framework in which the army maintained its role as the most significant political actor in Indonesia. However, the violent confrontations over the land reform question in the 1960s clearly showed that this ambitious balancing act was becoming increasingly unstable. For all their progress in the 1950s and early 1960s – they were now the largest communist party outside of the official communist nations – the PKI had been unsuccessful in two important respects: they had failed to penetrate the upper echelons of the state bureaucracy, and they had failed to offset the army's adamant opposition to its domestic activities.[24] The attempt to break the army's monopoly on armed force by arming the peasantry has since been interpreted as a tacit acknowledgement of the impossibility of persuading the army to set aside their objections to the PKI's programme.[25] The PKI's continued progress would be contingent upon a preservation of the delicate balance of power which Sukarno had managed throughout the 'Guided Democracy' years. By the summer of 1965, it was patently clear that the present arrangement was considered unsatisfactory by the Indonesian army, and it was in this atmosphere of mutual suspicion that rumours of an anti-communist coup began to circulate in August and September.

The 30th September Movement/The 'Attempted Coup'

To this day, the precise details of what happened in Indonesia on the night of 30th September 1965 remain far from clear. In particular, the exact nature of the operation, who instigated it and with what end in mind, all remain shrouded in considerable uncertainty.

A certain amount of factual detail is clear beyond any serious doubt. Early in the morning of 1st October 1965, a group of middle-ranking offers, led by Lieutenant Colonel Untung, set about attempting to kidnap seven of the army's most senior Generals. General Yani and two other Generals, Haryono and Panjaitan, were killed at their houses after resisting arrest. Three others, Parman, Suprapto and Sutojo, were successfully abducted and taken to a secret location at Lubang Buaya, south of Jakarta, where they were killed by members of the PKI youth group *Pemuda Rakyat*, possibly in the presence of members of the PKI women's section, *Gerwani*. The plotters failed to kidnap General Nasution, instead mistakenly capturing his unfortunate aide, who was also murdered at Lubang Buaya. The bodies of all seven were thrown down a well. Nasution was wounded in the attempted abduction, but managed to flee to safety. His young daughter, Ade Irma Suryani, was caught in the crossfire and fatally wounded by a gunshot.

The conspirators announced themselves, by radio broadcast, as the

'30th September Movement', and explained their actions as a pre-emptive measure to prevent the overthrow of President Sukarno by a 'Council of Generals' backed by the US Central Intelligence Agency (CIA). The conspirators were motivated by a revulsion at the senior Generals' corruption, and what they considered to be the Generals' decline into decadent luxuriousness, as well as professional grievances concerning the perceived poor performance of their superiors. This mutiny would come to be referred to as an 'attempted coup' in much of the subsequent discourse although, as we shall see, the description is by no means satisfactory. By the early hours of 2nd October, the '30th September Movement' had been defeated in Jakarta (there was a more prolonged struggle in Central Java, where the Indonesian army took about three more weeks to defeat a rebellion affiliated with the '30th September Movement'). General Suharto, excluded from the conspirators' list of targets in the mistaken belief that he was an apolitical figure who would adjust to the changed circumstances, led the army's strategic reserve, Kostrad, in a counter-offensive which quickly outmanoeuvred the rebellious battalions of the '30th September Movement'. By this point, however, the PKI had apparently thrown its support behind the abortive Movement; a PKI march in Jogjakarta declared its support for the Movement, and the party's Jakarta daily newspaper, *Harian Rakjat*, published an editorial which, though describing it as an internal army affair, none the less offered fulsome praise for the Movement.

It is by no means certain that the conspirators originally intended to kill their victims. In Indonesia, the practice of kidnapping and roughing-up political opponents in order to bully them into acquiescence was not uncommon. It is reasonably likely that the conspirators panicked when some of the Generals resisted arrest, and that the bloodshed was not an original part of the plan. In any event, the killings were the first political assassinations in Indonesia since the war of independence, and they shocked a conservative nation. The nature and extent of the PKI's involvement remains unclear to this day. That the PKI offered vocal support for the Movement there is little doubt; Untung and the plotters also received assistance from PKI-affiliated transport and communications unions on 1st October. However, it is significant that the PKI made no attempt to rally its considerable mass membership behind the Movement – a step which would have been eminently sensible if the party had really been behind the 'coup'. It would have been obvious to the PKI that the party was not in a position to take on the army in a physical confrontation, and that support for an internal army *putsch* would risk triggering such a confrontation. The PKI had been making steady gains from its policy of co-operation with non-communist forces, and it seems unlikely that the party would have deliberately risked all on a short-term and highly dangerous programme of insurrection. The decision to throw the party's weight behind the Movement appears to have been made by a handful of individuals in the very top echelons of the party, with Aidit coming to the conclusion that involving the party in the 30th September Movement without actually providing physical support (apart from the participation of a number of *Pemuda Rakyat* members) would allow the PKI the opportunity to rid itself of its main opposition (the right-wing Generals) without soiling its hands.[26]

Irrespective of the involvement of certain senior PKI individuals, and the PKI's sympathetic stance towards the Movement in its immediate wake (this would soon be revised for pragmatic reasons), the Movement was primarily an internal rebellion by middle-ranking officers, and they were the central actors in the drama. In this context, Damien Kingsbury observes the inadequacy of the 'coup' label to describe the activities of the 30th September Movement – given that the 'coup' was intended to protect President Sukarno and protect the status quo, the Movement does not match up comfortably with accepted notions of what a 'coup' normally entails. Sukarno would later be accused, with little solid evidence, of direct involvement in planning the 'coup' – in effect, of plotting a coup to overthrow himself.[27] The Movement itself was composed of two groups: one group was mainly young Central Javanese officers who were opposed to the corruption and Westernisation epitomised by the Nasution faction, but were also anti-communist; the other group comprised older Air Force officers, opportunists who were concerned about reductions in the military budget and were dependent on Sukarno remaining in power to prolong their careers. Neither group was Marxist, but both were prepared to use the support of the PKI in order to help achieve their respective aims.[28] As Harold Crouch observes in his seminal work, *The Army and Politics in Indonesia*, the evidence put forward at the subsequent trial of the 30th September plotters does not suggest that Untung and his colleagues were conscious agents of the PKI – they were motivated by their own concerns, independent of the PKI. The main initiative for the 30th September movement appears to have come from these 'progressive officers', with the PKI latching on to them at the last moment.[29]

A detailed study of the 30th September Movement appears in John Roosa's recent book, *Pretext for Mass Murder: The September 30th Movement & Suharto's Coup D'Etat in Indonesia* (2006). Correctly identifying the movement as a 'tangled, incoherent mess'[30], Roosa outlines four different interpretations of the Movement. The Movement could be seen variously as (a) an attempt by the PKI, as an institution, to seize power; (b) an internal army *putsch* by junior officers; (c) an internal army matter with the PKI playing a large supporting role; or (d) a movement organised by double-agents through Suharto and Nasution, with the aim of discrediting the PKI and facilitating Suharto's seizure of power.[31] The first and fourth options are the least plausible for want of evidence of the active involvement of either the PKI or Suharto in planning the events of 30th September. Peter Dale Scott has, however, identified a number of startling elements in the execution of the plot and its repression that may hint at the connivance or complicity of the Suharto clique that ultimately came to power: the failure of the rebellious battalions to guard the one side of Jakarta's Merdeka Square on which the headquarters of the army's strategic forces were situated appears to be as suspicious as the fact that the conspirators only targeted those generals who might have challenged Suharto's assumption of power.[32] Interestingly, in Jakarta and Central Java, the very battalions that had supplied the rebellious companies were also used to put down the rebellion. Two-thirds of one paratroop brigade, plus one company and one platoon, constituted the whole of the Movement's force in Jakarta. Two of these companies (the 454th and 530th battalions) were elite raiders who had been among the main recipients of US military aid. These supplied the bulk of the troops who put down the rebellion in Jakarta.[33] The bulk of the army's personnel for the parallel 'coup' in Central Java came from the Diponegoro division, which had a prominent role in operating two shipping companies established by Suharto and his political associate Bob Hassan. The latter had been the commissioning agent in a US deal to deliver 200 light aircraft to the Indonesian Army in July 1965; as well as supplying the bulk of the 'coup' personnel in Java, this division also provided the bulk of the personnel for its suppression.[34] On balance, however, this evidence, mostly circumstantial if highly suspicious, is not sufficient to establish active involvement on the part of Suharto in the 30th September Movement (option (d), above). There is little concrete evidence in support of this position; likewise the allegation that the PKI instigated the proceedings is equally unsupported.

We shall probably never know the whole truth about the 30th September Movement – Suharto's regime has subsequently 'boobytrapped the historians' path with false clues, dead-end diversions, and doctored bits of evidence'.[35] Although unanswered questions remain with respect to the Movement's poor design and the basis of the plotters' commonality[36], a combination of the second and third interpretations, (b) and (c) above, appears to represent the most plausible scenario. In this context, a degree of tacit support and encouragement – stopping short, as far as the available evidence indicates, of active connivance – from the right-wing Generals, would have accorded with their ultimate aim of helping to induce a 'coup' in order to eliminate their rivals at the army's centre, and pave the way for the elimination of the civilian left.[37] In a subsequent statement, the PKI's former Secretary General Sudisman attributed the PKI's involvement to a handful of PKI leaders who, as individuals, decided to support the rebellious officers in order to counter the right-wing army Generals who were obstructing the PKI's implementation of its domestic programmes (see 'The PKI', above), as well as threatening to overthrow Sukarno.[38] Given the tense stand-off between the PKI and the army, Aidit would have been concerned about the possible overthrow of Sukarno, which would have left the PKI unprotected against any army move to purge the top levels of government and the military of all PKI officials. A successful coup carried out by the Council of Generals would have meant overturning Sukarnoist and communist influence in Indonesia's ongoing national revolution, amounting, in effect, to a 'counter-revolution'. Sukarno himself was seriously ill in the summer of 1965 (he had been suffering from blackouts and fainting fits), and rumours abounded that the country's venerated President – the man who stood between the Indonesian army and the PKI – would be dead in a matter of weeks, leaving the way free for an army takeover. Desperate to pre-empt such a coup, but equally aware that an attempt to call out the masses for a demonstration or uprising would incur the risk of reprisals and risk the lives of the unarmed party masses, Aidit instead threw in his lot with the progressive officers and their 30th September Movement.[39]

Sukarno, perhaps sensing that the senior Generals would capitalise on the new development to discredit his policy of co-operation with the PKI, sought to play down the significance of the 30th September Movement, describing it as a mere 'ripple in the ocean of the [Indonesian national] revolution'.[40] The army, however, was determined to seize its opportunity to eliminate the PKI. The army-run newspapers ascribed to the 30th September Movement a new label, *Gestapu* – a tenuous acronym for '*Ge*rakan *Ti*ga *Pu*luh September' ('thirtieth of September Movement'), designed to evoke comparisons with the Gestapo of Nazi Germany. No sooner had Suharto's strategic reserve restored order in Jakarta, than a full-blown propaganda campaign was launched, with one fundamental aim: to depict the army mutiny of 30th September 1965 (now routinely referred to as 'Gestapu') as a Chinese-backed communist coup attempt aimed at overthrowing the Indonesian state and installing a foreign-backed, atheistic and communistic dictatorship, in total violation of *Pancasila*, *Nasakom*, and everything that the Indonesian state stood for. This in turn would provide the pretext for the wholesale destruction of the PKI which the right-wing Generals had long hoped to achieve.

Notes
1 Sukarno did not have separate first and second names. His full name is Sukarno. The same is true of other important figures in recent Indonesian history, including Generals Suharto and Sukendro.
2 For the first two sections of this chapter ('Indonesia 1950-57' and 'Guided Democracy'), I have drawn heavily from M Rickleffs, *A History of Modern Indonesia Since 1200* (Basingstoke: Palgrave, 2001) Chapters 19 & 20.
3 Indonesia's Muslims were divided into two distinct sections: the more pious,

'Constructive Bloodbath' in Indonesia

practising Muslims (*santri*), and those whose religious affiliation was considered merely 'nominal' (*abangan*).

4 Rudolf Mrazek, *Sjahrir: Politics and Exile in Indonesia* (Ithaca, New York: Cornell University Southeast Asia Program, 1994) p455, cited in John Roosa, *Pretext for Mass Murder: The September 30th Movement & Suharto's Coup D'Etat in Indonesia* (Madison: University of Wisconsin Press, 2006), p185.

5 At the time, many people suspected that the assasination attempt had been deliberately staged by Sukarno supporters in order to provide a pretext for maintaining 'Guided Democracy'.

6 Peter Edman, *Communism A La Aidit: The Indonesian Communist Party Under DN Aidit*, 1950-1965, Townsville: James Cook University, 1987) pp11-12.

7 Ibid, p116.

8 Ibid, p26.

9 Jacques Leclerc, *Aidit and the Problem of the Party in 1950* (Unpublished), p33, cited in Edman, *Communism A La Aidit*, p41.

10 DN Aidit, 'The Road to a People's Democracy for Indonesia' in Aidit, *Selected Works Vol 1* (Jakarta, Jajaan Pembaruan,1959), pp174-175, cited in Edman, *Communism A La Aidit*, p43.

11 Aidit, 'The National United Front and Its History' in *Selected Works Vol 1*, p54, cited in Edman, *Communism A La Aidit*, p43.

12 Edman, *Communism A La Aidit*, p52.

13 National China News Agency (NCNA), Dec 6, 1963, cited in Sheldon W. Simon, *The Broken Triangle: Peking, Djakarta, and the PKI* (Baltimore: John Hopkins Press, 1969), p39.

14 Report Developed at Higher Party School of the CP Central Committee, Sep 2, 1963 (Peking: Foreign Languages Press, 1964) pp34-37, cited in Simon, *Broken Triangle*, p77.

15 DN Aidit, 'The Future of the Indonesian Peasant Movement', *Selected Writings* vol I p114. 69-70, cited in Edman, *Communism A La Aidit*, pp69-70

16 Edman, *Communism A La Aidit*, p71.

17 Ibid, p73.

18 Ibid, p77.

19 Ibid, p80.

20 Ibid, p80.

21 *Harian Rajkat* (daily newspaper), July 9 1965, cited in Simon, *Broken Triangle*, p84.

22 Simon, *Broken Triangle*, p103.

23 D Hindley, *The Communist Party of Indonesia* (Berkeley: University of California Press, 1964) pp286-297, cited in Damien Kingsbury, *The Politics of Indonesia* (Oxford: Oxford University Press, 1998), p59.

24 Simon, *Broken Triangle*, p103.

25 Robert Cribb and Colin Brown, *Modern Indonesia: A History Since 1945* (New York: Longman, 1995), p95.

26 Edman, *Communism A La Aidit*, p101.

27 Damien Kingsbury, *The Politics of Indonesia* (Oxford: Oxford Univesrsity Press, 1998), p62.
28 Gabriel Kolko – *Confronting the Third World: United States Foreign Policy 1945 – 1980* (New York: Pantheon, 1988), p178.
29 Harold Crouch, *The Army and Politics in Indonesia* (Singapore: Equinox, 2007), pp104-105.
30 Roosa, *Pretext for Mass Murder*, p61.
31 Ibid, p62.
32 Peter Dale Scott, 'The United States and the Overthrow of Sukarno, 1965-67', *Pacific Affairs*, Vol 58, No 2 (Summer, 1985), pp239-274, p242.
33 Ibid, p243.
34 Ibid, p257.
35 Roosa, *Pretext for Mass Murder*, p81.
36 Ibid, p74.
37 Peter Dale Scott, 'The United States and the Overthrow of Sukarno, 1965-67', p239.
38 Sudisman, *Analysis of Responsibility*, Melbourne: Works Cooperative, 1975, p7, cited in Roosa, *Pretext for Mass Murder*, p141
39 Roosa, *Pretext for Mass Murder*, p158.
40 Sukarno's speech, 16th October 1965, cited in Crouch, *Army and Politics*, p162.

CHAPTER TWO

'Pursue, Purge and Destroy'

The Massacre of the PKI

From the moment that the 30th September Movement's defeat was confirmed on 2nd October 1965, the Indonesian army turned its attention to the implementation of a nationwide propaganda blitz against the PKI which, the army claimed, had instigated the so-called 'Gestapu' affair. PKI members would be identified as traitors and thugs, and religion would be invoked in order to incite the country's Muslims into action, preying on their religious sensibilities by raising the spectre of a takeover by militant atheists, which would presumably have disastrous implications for the religious community. The message of the campaign was not limited either to calling for the prosecution of the ringleaders of the 'Gestapu' or to a generic denunciation of the PKI. Instead, the army newspapers incited physical violence against PKI members in unequivocal terms, with a strong emphasis on a sense of religious duty. An editorial in the army newspaper *Angkatan Bersendjata* on 8th October issued a clear call to arms: 'The sword cannot be met by the Koran ... but must be met by the sword. The Koran itself says that whoever opposes you should be opposed as they oppose you.' A few days later, the same newspaper would proclaim: 'God is with us because we are on the path that is right and that he has set for us'.[1] Joining this chorus of army-sponsored calls for the physical elimination of the PKI, a sensationalist newspaper, *Api Pancasila*, appeared in circulation just days after the coup, and disappeared again soon after the slaughter; the mysterious timing of its publication and subsequent disappearance have prompted suggestions that the American CIA was involved in its production and dissemination.[2] The PKI had twice recovered from concerted campaigns against it: during the years of foreign occupation, and later after the Madiun uprising, the party was driven underground, only to subsequently re-emerge. The nature and scale of this latest crackdown would eclipse the repression after Madiun, with the army absolutely determined that the PKI would be unable to recover this time.

Deception was central to the army's campaign against the PKI. Army newspapers ran stories which featured a host of sordid – and completely false – details about the circumstances surrounding the murder of the Generals at Lubang Buaya. Their accounts alleged that, prior to the killings, a number of women from the PKI women's organisation, *Gerwani*, stripped naked and performed a lascivious dance in front of PKI cadres and air force officers involved in the 30th September Movement, before proceeding to a ritual genital mutilation of the Generals. The Generals' genitals were severed, and their eyes gouged out, before they were finally killed and their bodies disposed of. The *Gerwani* women celebrated by abandoning themselves to an orgy with PKI members and air force officers in attendance; the PKI leader, Aidit, awarded medals to the most depraved performers.[3] In every detail – save for the killing – this account was a complete fabrication, yet it was circulated deliberately by the army. If the allegations in relation to genital mutilation would have been shocking enough in most cultures, the descriptions of naked dancing and wild group sex were designed to shock the sensibilities of a highly conservative society, and reinforce the notion that the communists represented a way of life that was anathema to traditional Indonesian values.

When the Generals' bodies were discovered, the visible effects of decomposition were interpreted as corroboration of the allegations of mutilation. A subsequent autopsy would determine that the generals had not been mutilated at all – in the short term, however, the impact of these false accounts was explosive. In the eyes, in particular, of the country's *santri* (zealous) Muslim community – already hardly well-disposed towards the PKI – the accounts merely confirmed their suspicions about the PKI, and provided a firm, state-approved justification to pursue their long-standing vendetta in a more open and violent manner than had hitherto been feasible. On the occasion of the funeral of Nasution's young daughter Irma, accidentally killed by a gunshot on the night of the 'coup attempt' of 30th September, the Navy chief Admiral Eddy Martadinata is reported to have passed on a message to Muslim student leaders, instructing them to 'sikat' – literally 'sweep', 'clean up' or 'wipe out'. The connection between the 'coup attempt' of 30th September and the incipient anti-PKI purge would later be made explicit by General Nasution in an address to a student gathering: 'Since they have committed treason, they must be destroyed and quarantined from all activities in our fatherland.'[4] In retribution for the activities of the plotters of 30th September, the entire PKI membership – hundreds of thousands of people, most of whom knew absolutely nothing about the 'coup' – 'should no longer be protected by the law', but should instead be 'immediately smashed'.[5] The Muslim youth groups, who had waited for years for an opportunity such as this, did not disappoint the army Generals. They would comprise the vanguard in the anti-communist massacre, with the Indonesian army orchestrating and providing essential logistical support for the killings, in a systematic campaign of mass murder which would last several months and leave upwards of half a million people dead. In certain regions, the killing would be carried out by equally zealous members of other religious faiths – namely Hindus (in Bali) and Catholics (in Sumatra and the Lesser Sundas). The focus in the ensuing pages is on Java and Bali, on account of the greater preponderance of evidence in relation to those islands; the massacres would, however, claim victims in other parts of the archipelago, most notably North Sumatra, where the PKI had become a strong political force. Tens of thousands of people, mostly Javanese plantation workers, were murdered in North Sumatra.

The Massacre – Jakarta and Central Java

The earliest stages of the campaign were characterised by non-violent administrative measures aimed at suspending the legal operation of the PKI's existing political machinery. Fifty-seven communist MPs were 'suspended', and over a hundred members of the so-called Provisional People's Deliberative Assembly (MPRS) were banned for suspected complicity in the 'Gestapu' affair. A thorough purge of communists in government departments resulted in 1,371 dismissals in the maritime ministry alone. The official news agency, Antara, was placed under military control in order to neutralise its perceived pro-communist bias, and dozens of reporters were arrested and detained for interrogation. It was only a matter of days, however, before the campaign descended into open and systematic violence, precipitated by a significant power shift in the highest echelon of state power in the immediate wake of the 30th September events. On 1st October, Sukarno issued an order appointing Major General Pranoto, a Sukarno loyalist, to the position of Army Chief of Staff; in an unprecedented move, this appointment was rejected outright by Suharto, with the support of Nasution. The army leadership had passed to Suharto after the elimination of Yani and the other leading generals on 30th September. Suharto and Nasution had been among the senior officers who had expressed concerns about the reluctance of Yani and his colleagues to confront Sukarno over the rise of the PKI; they did not wish to see responsibility for dealing with 'Gestapu' entrusted to a man so closely associated with Sukarno's PKI-friendly policies. After a five-hour meeting on 2nd October, Suharto agreed to accept Pranoto's appointment, on condition that the latter's role would be confined to ordinary 'daily tasks', while Suharto would be given responsibility for the 'restoration of security and order'. In form, this was a compromise – in substance, however, it marked a crucial shift in power, with the Suharto-Nasution clique effectively dictating terms to Sukarno, wresting control from the President for the duration of the crisis and, ultimately, beyond.[6] Suharto took over formal control of the army a fortnight later, using it as a vehicle for his accession to the presidency.

Conscious that Sukarno retained a considerable support base within the army, Suharto was wary that any overt orders instructing mass arrests or killings of PKI members might trigger a divisive confrontation, with regional army commanders being asked to choose between the President and the Suharto-Nasution group. Suharto therefore set about initiating the anti-communist purge by more subtle means, with instructions conveyed informally to local military commanders. The discretion accordingly conferred upon regional military leaders offers one explanation for the apparent variation in the nature and scale of the anti-PKI measures from place to place.[7] The main military instrument for the exercise of state power by the new Suharto-Nasution regime was KOPKAMTIB (Operational Command for the Restoration of Security and Order), an intelligence and security command network extending from Suharto down to local military commanders at the village level. Assured by the Suharto clique that they could proceed with impunity, anti-PKI civilians launched their first mass action on 8th October 1965, when an anti-PKI mob, mainly composed of members of Muslim youth organisations, attacked the PKI's Jakarta headquarters and set it ablaze. In Java, where a group linked with the 'Gestapu' movement had launched a similar coup on 30th September led by Colonel Suherman, troops from the army's Special Force (RPKAD) section began arming and training anti-communist youth groups for the specific purpose of destroying the PKI.[8] In tandem with the Muslim youth groups, the army tracked down PKI members using membership lists obtained from the ransacking of PKI offices. Party leadership and rank and file alike were targeted.

A leading figure in the army-led operation was Lieutenant-General Sarwo Edhie. On 26th October, Sarwo Edhie held a meeting of the Joint Security Staff at the military command staff office in the Surakarta district in Java. By 23rd October, the last remnants of resistance of the 30th September Movement had been defeated in Central Java; nevertheless, Sarwo Edhie emphasised the need to press on and intensify the campaign against the Movement, which should 'be given no opportunity to concentrate'; the communists should 'be pushed back systematically by all means, including *psywar*, distribution of pamphlets and the spreading of information to achieve the goal of *slowing down* [PKI activities].'[9] 'Psywar' – psychological warfare – had played a central part in inciting popular feeling against the PKI, furnishing the army with the twin benefits of political support and civilian participation in their campaign against the PKI. The steady stream of anti-PKI propaganda, combining appeals to both nationalist and religious sentiment, would not abate in the months ahead. In a deliberate attempt to rouse the ire of nationalists, the new regime exploited the strong links between the PKI and the communist government in Peking to portray the 30th September Movement as a foreign-backed conspiracy and hence an encroachment upon Indonesia's sovereignty, with Nasution claiming that Aidit was 'directly or indirectly assisted by a foreign country'.[10]

In his later recollections, Sarwo Edhie emphasised the role played by the Muslim youth groups in Java. The geographical area was too big and too crowded for an effective distribution of military forces: 'We decided to encourage the anti-communist civilians to help with the job. In Solo we gathered together the youth, the nationalist groups, the religious organisations. We gave them two or three days' training, then sent them out to kill the communists'.[11] Meanwhile, anti-communist informers led troops in Central Java to specific villages and individuals whom they alleged were communists. By late October, a veritable tide of violence was sweeping across the cities and the countryside. The victims were PKI members of all ranks, as well as many individuals with no links to the PKI – peasants, for example, who had incurred the displeasure of Muslim landlords by asking for lower rents. The victims included members of religious minorities disliked by the Muslim groups and, in some very rare cases, apolitical people who had been denounced by personal enemies wishing to settle a score. Although the killings were carried out by relatively technologically unsophisticated methods – there would be no gas chambers in Indonesia, just traditional knives or broad-bladed sickles (where the executioners were civilians) and gunfire (where the executioners were soldiers) – the killing was nevertheless carried out with industrial efficiency. In the coastal town of Cirebon in Java, residents reported that the killers set up a guillotine that worked steadily throughout the day, day after day.[12] From Salatiga in Eastern Java, an American correspondent provided the *Washington Post* with a grim account of a typical massacre:

> 'At each building, an army captain read names from a list, advising them of their guilt "in the name of the law". Eventually filled with 60 prisoners and piloted by a platoon of troops, the trucks drove six miles through a dark landscape of rice fields and rubber estates to a barren spot near the village of Djelok. The neighbourhood peasants had been ordered by their headman to dig a large pit the day before. The prisoners, lined up at the edge of the pit, were shot down in a matter of minutes. Some may have been buried alive.'[13]

Much of the contemporary and subsequent writing on the killings portrayed them as a spontaneous response to the atrocities committed by the 30th September plotters. However, as Benedict Anderson and Ruth McVey observed in their detailed study of the killings, there was a significant time lapse between the 'coup' of 30th September and the beginning of large-scale, organised killing of alleged communists. Noting that, after 30th September, 'three weeks elapsed in which no violence or trace of civil war occurred, even according to the Army itself', Anderson and McVey concluded that the 30th September affair and the subsequent anti-communist campaign 'form *quite separate political phenomena*'.[14] In the media discourse at the time, however, the two were quite deliberately conflated, with the term 'Gestapu' being used to refer both to the September 30th conspirators and to the PKI mass membership who were targeted in the anti-communist campaign.

Running parallel to the anti-communist purge was a campaign of violence against the country's Chinese community. The Chinese community was resented in many quarters on account of its relatively privileged economic position, and the official portrayal of the 30th September affair as having been instigated by the guiding hand of the People's Republic of China (PRC) further fuelled anti-Chinese feeling. The Chinese had no one to protect them; Sukarno and the PKI were respectively discredited and under attack, and the Chinese government was powerless due to its geographical distance.[15] This campaign also benefited from overt military sanction – Sumitro, the regional commander of the East Kalimantan province, announced that 'shops run by Chinese nationals, including even their stocks and equipment', would be confiscated by February 1967.[16] The anti-Chinese violence was opportunist in nature and was not directly linked with the Generals' anti-communist campaign, accounting for only a tiny percentage of the victims of 1965-66. The pogroms none the less fitted neatly into the new regime's official framework justifying the large-scale violence of the October 1965 to March 1966 period, perhaps most neatly exemplified by Adam Malik's assertion that the failure of 'Gestapu', and the subsequent violence, 'meant the liberation of Indonesia from PRC domination in the ideological field, which in turn meant the liberation of Indonesia from communist dictatorship and personality cult'.[17] Malik was a prominent supporter of Suharto who became a senior minister in the post-1965 government.

One distinctive trait of the entire campaign was the attempt to provide a veneer of legality and procedural propriety to an operation which, being committed to a programme of mass summary extra-judicial execution, was inherently illegal and barbaric. The Generals included among their number many men who had been educated in the West, and they were well aware of the importance of maintaining some semblance of respect for legal norms, however tenuously constructed. The announcement by military men that their actions were 'in the name of the law' should be seen in this light, as should the issuing to detainees of paperwork containing, by way of explanation for their arrest, the stock phrase 'directly or indirectly involved in the September 30th Movement'.[18] Indeed, Nasution's declaration that the entire PKI mass membership had 'committed treason' also borrows from the language of criminal justice in order to give a sense of legitimacy to the army's subsequent actions. Many years later, the man with overall responsibility for the campaign, General Suharto, would be rather more candid about the nature and aims of the campaign – the strategy, he wrote, was to 'pursue, purge and destroy'.[19] The beleaguered President Sukarno, who would remain in nominal charge of the country for some time while effective power was exercised by the Suharto-Nasution military clique, protested in vain that the army's campaign against the PKI constituted a disproportionate response to the 30th September affair. The army, Sukarno protested on 27th October, was 'burning down a house to kill a rat'.[20] His pleas fell on deaf ears, as the army proceeded with a campaign which recognised, on the question of guilt, no distinction between the highest officials of the PKI and those ordinary party members who, in the terminology of the new regime, were 'indirectly' involved in the September 30th Movement by virtue of their membership of the party.

In November, the army managed to track down the PKI leader Aidit. Aidit, who had been in hiding for several weeks since the 30th September mutiny, was arrested on 22nd November 1965. Colonel Yasir Hadibroto, a KOSTRAD commander dispatched by Suharto to Central Java with express instructions to 'deal with' Aidit, ordered his men to strap up the communist leader, stand him in front of a well, and shoot him dead. Aidit's body was thrown down a well, covered with leaves and burnt, and banana trees planted over the site. Two days later, Yasir met Suharto in Jogjakarta. According to Yasir's personal account, Yasir asked Suharto 'Is this what you meant when you said we should "deal with" him?' and Suharto merely smiled and said nothing.[21] The death of Aidit would not lead to a reduction, still less a cessation, of the anti-communist violence. Only in West Java, which was regarded as a stronghold of Muslim militancy, did the army discourage vigilante killings, as it did not wish to furnish the Muslim youth groups with weaponry in that region. The numbers of deaths in West Java were therefore significantly lower than in the other Javanese provinces.

Despite the army's resources, and despite the willing participation of the Muslim and nationalist youth, the task of physically eliminating the entire PKI mass membership presented serious logistical challenges. Mass arrests and detentions provided an interim solution – tens of thousands of Indonesians would remain in detention well into the 1970s. Survivors' accounts speak of vicious interrogation sessions in which prisoners were beaten and intimidated. The personal account of one survivor, a woman named Bu Yeti, describes her experience in a police station cell in Kuningan, South Jakarta, in November 1965. Prisoners were instructed to take off their shirts before being repeatedly kicked with spiked boots and beaten with belts. Once they had fainted from loss of blood, they would be dragged back to their cells.[22] While the pursuit of the PKI in Central Java and Jakarta was relentless, the bloodiest violence took place in East Java and on the island of Bali.

East Java

In East Java, the PKI's active political support for land reform, combined with their efforts at enforcing the new land reforms laws of 1959-60, incurred the bitter enmity of the influential Muslim landlords. Orthodox Muslims in East Java were also offended by the PKI's association with the Kejawen branch of Islam, a distinctive interpretation which blended Hindu and animist elements, and was viewed by orthodox Muslims as a form of blasphemy bordering on black magic.[23] In a detailed study focusing on the district of Kediri, Kenneth R. Young emphasises the importance of social history in explaining the background to the mutual antipathy between Muslim and communist elements in East Java.[24]

The unresolved tensions between the orthodox (*santri*) and nominal (*abangan*) Muslims derived from Kediri's experience during the Dutch colonial period, when the region was opened up for exploitation by Dutch plantation interests, most notably in sugar production. A stream of migrants were attracted to the region, with the result that a high proportion (roughly 40%) of villagers acquired no land, and had to work as wage labourers, setting in place significant and visible class differences within the immigrant communities.[25] The immigrants from the north coast asserted their identity through closer adherence to Islam, establishing distinctively *santri* communities which contrasted sharply with the adjacent *abangan* communities, who hailed from central Java. Although the latter identified themselves with the PKI, it was their connection with black magic and irreligious practices which comprised the primary reason for the friction with *santri* Muslims. These divisions were only intensified under the system of parliamentary democracy of 1950-57.[26] The situation became increasingly confrontational in the early 1960s. In 1961, the PKI-affiliated peasant organisation BTI occupied sugar mills in Jengkol. About three thousand peasants participated in this action, which finally ended when the army ejected the peasants, at a cost of twenty-four casualties. Meanwhile, PKI-backed squatters had successfully held on to land occupied in the former Dutch upland estates.[27]

In response to these developments, and prompted in particular by the PKI's campaigns for the enforcement of the Crop Sharing Law and the Basic Agrarian Law (*aksi sepihak* – unilateral or 'direct' actions), the landlords in Kediri mobilised resistance through the PNI and NU parties.[28] In October 1965, after the provocation of 'Gestapu' and upon receipt of the signal to act from the military authorities, these organisations – in particular the black-shirted militant Ansor youth of the NU party – would be at the forefront of the campaign in East Java, motivated as much by economic and political grievances arising from the land reform issue as by religious and ideological sentiment. In October 1965, widely-circulated leaflets implored Muslims to remember the 'thousands of Muslims [who] were murdered by the other side' at Madiun in 1948.[29] The regional leaders of the Muslim youth group Ansor met in East Java and agreed to hold a 'Vigilance Rally of Godly People', a series of coordinated rallies in a number of towns, on 13th October. The Ansor leaders agreed that the rallies would culminate in physical attacks on local PKI headquarters and staff.[30] During the rally on 13th October, eleven

PKI members were hacked to death trying to defend the party headquarters. The rally marked the beginning of widespread violence in Kediri and the surrounding regions. In the town of Pare, some Ansor leaders attempted to protect their PKI-affiliated peasants by giving them Ansor or NU badges; when one of the peasants, in a nervous panic, identified himself as a PKI member, all three hundred peasants were killed, and an atmosphere of mutual distrust arose within Ansor itself.[31] In the southern sub-district of Wates, PKI members gathered in large numbers – about ten thousand in all – in order to march to safety in Madiun. They were attacked by a combination of army and Ansor elements, and 1,200 people were killed before they were subdued and arrested.[32]

There are relatively few first-hand accounts of the killing from Indonesians. A culture of secrecy has surrounded the killings, reinforced by the oppressive authoritarianism of the Suharto regime, with eyewitnesses unwilling to speak about the killings for fear of violent retribution from Muslim elements, or of victimisation by an authoritarian state that was unwilling to have the issue discussed in any open context, and was inclined to interpret any discussion as tantamount to a declaration of sympathy for the detested PKI. One outstanding study was, however, conducted in the years shortly after the killings. It comprised a number of detailed eyewitness accounts, necessarily anonymous in view of the repressive conditions imposed by the fledgling Suharto dictatorship. The document – 'Additional Data on Counter-Revolutionary Cruelty in Indonesia, Especially in East Java'[33], provides some idea of the sort of wantonly sadistic violence employed by the Muslim youth groups in their purported defence of 'godliness'.

In Lwang, in the East Java province of Malang, a gang comprising members of the Muslim youth organisation Ansor led their victims to specially-prepared holes near the town's botanical gardens. Victims were taken to the holes one by one, and nooses were placed around their necks and tightened until they collapsed. The victims were then beaten to death with iron rods and other hard implements, and subsequently decapitated.[34] In the Malang town of Singosari, an Ansor gang attacked a young boy who was the son of a local committee member. He was tied to a jeep and dragged behind it until he was dead; both his parents subsequently committed suicide.[35] In Jember, over a three-month period, victims were transported on trucks belonging to the state-owned plantation corporation PN Perkebunan, and taken to the rubber plantations of Wonogiri and Glantangan, and the Nglangan coconut plantation. The victims were buried in large holes, with about ten to fifteen bodies in each hole.[36]

In the town of Nglekok in the Blitar district, a leading figure in the local *Gerwani* branch was killed, along with her husband, a man named Djumadi. They had been married only thirty-five days. She was raped many times by an Ansor gang, who slit her body open from her breasts to her vulva.[37] In the same town, a man named Nursamsu was dismembered, and pieces of his body were hung in the homes of his friends.[38] In Garum, a *Gerwani* member named Ny Jajus was attacked by an Ansor gang. She was pregnant at the time of the attack – her attackers cut open her body before she was killed. Her husband, a man named Pak Djajus, had his face sliced with a dagger repeatedly until he died.[39] In Pare in Kediri, the headmaster of a local high school – a man named Suranto – was murdered after meeting his pregnant wife, who had been at a meeting of an *arisan* (a rotating credit and social club) of which she was a member. On their way home, the couple were beaten until they fell unconscious, and then killed. The man's head was cut off, and his wife's stomach was cut open, the baby removed and cut to pieces. The couple's five young children – the oldest being only eleven years old – were forcibly left to fend for themselves, as Ansor members warned neighbours not to help them.[40] Genital mutilation features heavily in the accounts. Women would be killed by being stabbed through the vagina with long knives until their stomachs were pierced; their heads and breasts were cut off and displayed on roadside guard huts. Male victims would often have their penises severed.[41]

The worst slaughter in East Java took place in the Kediri district. The regional military commander in Kediri was the brother of General Sutojo, one of the generals killed in the 30th September mutiny; operations here were carried out with particular zeal. As the Muslim youth did not have the authority to order villagers to dig mass graves, individual victims were marched into fields and made to dig their own graves. Reports indicate that a number of people were buried alive.[42] As thousands of PKI members were being murdered by Ansor youths, the local Muslim leader, Hadji Makrus Ali, gave his blessing to the killings, explaining them as 'the will of God'.[43] It would be a mistake, however, to conceive of the killings, in their entirety, as a Muslim-run operation. As well as giving the Muslim groups every assurance that they could act with impunity, the army participated directly in the killing as far as it was practicable to do so. Looking back on the period, the commander of the army's East Java division, Major General Sumitro, was quite clear on this, proudly insisting that 'most local commanders did their utmost to kill as many cadres as possible'.[44] The timing of the violence strongly suggests that the arrival of RPKAD was the trigger for the violence in most areas, after a period of about a fortnight of relative calm after the 'coup' of 30th September. Nevertheless, the role of the Muslim groups – dictated as much by leadership figures within the community as by rank-and-file zealousness – was of great significance. In Pasuran, east of Surabaya, a two-week killing spree was initiated when the town's central mosque made a public announcement, demanding to know if the local Muslim men were really men, or 'only' women. Instigators posted lists of alleged communists at a local factory. A worker who had played guitar for the communist cultural group *Lekra* was beheaded, his head stuck on a pole outside the factory.[45] In December 1965, a horrified President Sukarno pleaded for the killers to at least observe the Muslim duty to respect the dead, who were being 'left under trees, beside rivers, thrown like the corpses of dead dogs'. Watching the fragile unity of his beloved nation disintegrating in a blaze of organised, violent savagery, Sukarno warned: 'If we go on as we are, brothers, we are going to hell, really we are going to hell.'[46] His pleas had little or no impact, and the killing progressed unabated until it petered out around March/April 1966, the momentum maintained by constant cheerleading from the Indonesian press – the gloating triumphalism of a *Suara Indonesia* editorial in December 1965 is not untypical: '[The communists] don't even need to see the red beret [of the RPKAD], it is enough simply to hear the roar of a truck, and the hearts of the big-shot G-30-S types begin to beat wildly with fear.'[47]

Bali

An estimated 80,000 people were killed in Bali alone – roughly 5% of a population of under two million – during the 1965-66 killings. The antagonisms on Bali reflected those in the nation at large, with the PKI espousing the cause of the peasantry via its peasant front, the BTI, in a vigorous campaign against the refusal of local landlords to abide by the new land reform laws. The PKI had also incurred the enmity of local religious groups – on Bali the major religion was, and remains, Hinduism – who were particularly affronted by the attempted desecration of a traditional Dewa Agung funeral in the Klungkung district by a group of PKI supporters.[48]

Troops from the Army Paracommando Regiment (RPKAD) and the East Java-based Brawijaya Division landed on the island in December 1965 to continue the task they had already begun in Central and East Java. As early as 5th October, published statements by the PNI and the local Muhammadiyah party made aggressive references to the need to restore order and 'crush the G-30-S traitors'. A statement by the Muhammadiyah party in the *Suara Indonesia* newspaper called on the people of Bali to 'assist all military forces in guarding public order and peace'. On 12th October, the PNI-affiliated Indonesian National School Pupils' Movement called on its members to 'work together with [the armed forces], and provide concrete assistance to [the armed forces] in annihilating G-30-S'.[49] Anti-PKI groups expressed concerns that the anti-PKI campaign in Bali was lagging behind the campaigns elsewhere in the archipelago. Addressing some fifty-thousand people at a Youth Day rally in Denpasar on 28th October, the PNI leader I Gusti Puto Merto called on Sukarno to order the 'cleansing' of the local government of PKI elements, and queried the relative inaction in Bali in comparison with the rest of the country.[50] On the same day, the Bali police commander, Major Ismono Ismakoen, issued a statement promising violent measures against anyone resisting the incipient anti-communist campaign: 'If there are still waverers in the economic, political, cultural, and social spheres, the police will not hesitate to take strong measures against them and, if necessary, to shoot them.'[51]

On 1st November, the local governor Suteja, after consultation with the local military commander Sjafiuddin, issued on order 'freezing' a limited number of PKI-affiliated mass organisations; Suteja also ordered the establishment of an 'inspection team' to investigate suspected 'Gestapu' activities in Bali. In early November, after his appointment as the regional KOPKAMTIB commander, Sjafiuddin publicly condemned the PKI and issued an instruction to mobilise the action to wipe it out. Meanwhile Suteja, who was himself strongly suspected of having PKI sympathies, was gradually pushed aside in response to open calls for his dismissal – he remained as nominal governor until 8th December, but had ceased to exercise any effective authority by about mid-November. Suteja's decline paved the way for a shift in local military support, away from Sukarno and in favour of the Suharto-Nasution clique. It was only in December, therefore, once the political and military forces at national and local levels were aligned, that the massacre could begin in earnest, with the *Suara Indonesia* newspaper confidently declaring: 'Now it is clear who is friend and who is foe'.[52] Until December, anti-communist actions had been confined to 'police actions' (*aksi-aksi polisionil*) against alleged communist sympathisers during November. Houses were burned, possessions stolen, and families intimidated by vigilante groups dressed in black and armed with swords, knives, cudgels and sometimes firearms. There were armed clashes between Pemuda Rakyat, Ansor and PNI supporters, sometimes also involving local police and military units, but relatively few killings.

Until December, the balance of local political forces was such that the PKI was operating from a position of relative security. The local military spent much of November preparing for the campaign, compiling lists of PKI members and fabricating documentation aimed at proving the complicity of Bali's communists in the 'Gestapu' affair. The same 'psychological warfare' methods which had been deployed so successfully in Java were also adopted here, with newspapers portraying PKI members as morally depraved and anti-religious. The army produced documentation which incriminated the Balinese PKI in plans to stage a local version of the 30th September 'coup'. The documentation indicated a sizeable unofficial PKI presence within the regional military command, including a list of about seventy-five low-to-middle-ranking army men. The documents also included details of plans to commit depraved acts, including the forced undressing of leading conservative political figures before a mass rally.[53] The *Suara Indonesia* newspaper also reported that the PKI's coup plans included an elaborate scheme whereby *Gerwani* members in Bali would sell themselves to army officers in order to buy weapons, so as to afford themselves the opportunity to castrate and murder the soldiers.[54]

The people of Bali were presented with a stark choice: they could either side with the state authorities in their anti-communist stand, or throw in their lot with the depraved and anti-religious PKI. Neutrality was not an option, as the *Suara* newspaper explained on 18th November when it warned that 'there are only two possible alternatives; to be on the side of the G-30-S or to stand behind the government in crushing the G-30-S. There is no such thing as a neutral position.'[55] This approach would manifest itself, in practice, in a logic of associative guilt exemplified by the murder of a night-market worker in the town of Kindamani. He was killed merely because he had once provided a storm lantern to a PKI rally after a power cut.[56] The district military commander Paidi emphasised that mere disavowal of the PKI would not be enough: 'Making a written statement is very easy; what matters most is real proof'.[57] In this context, the most effective way in which ordinary people could demonstrate their antipathy towards the PKI, and hence ensure their own personal safety, was to participate actively in the killings. Killing friends and acquaintances was also a way of mitigating against possible denunciations or accidental incrimination, as a survivor of the killings, Soe Hok Gie, explained: 'Survival is a very strong motive for action. To succeed, one has to cover one's tracks and leave no traces. Killing is the easiest and safest way to do this, because dead people do not speak.'[58] In this way, ordinary citizens were drawn in to the killing as a means of self-preservation.

A number of accounts of the killings present Bali as an exceptional case in which the army, unusually, acted to pacify the violence rather than instigate it.[59] This incorrect interpretation derives from a mistranslated quotation from Colonel Sarwo Edhie, who was reported to have commented, in December 1965: 'In Java we had to egg the people on to kill communists. In Bali we have to restrain them'. Reporters concluded that the mass killings occurred, as it were, organically, in response to the murder of an army officer and two

Ansor members by PKI youths in Jembrana on 30th November. However, with the army arriving so soon after this incident (in early December) it seems unlikely that a death toll in the tens of thousands would have been attributable to a mere two days' activity at the end of November (such widespread killing would in any case have been an implausible reaction to a relatively routine crime). A different, more plausible translation of Sarwo Edhie's full statement places a different interpretation on his comments: 'Whereas in Central Java I was concerned to crush the Gestapu, [in Bali] on the other hand, the people were already eager to crush the Gestapu to its roots. The important thing was not to let enthusiasm be misused by certain people, leading to anarchy. That is what we had to prevent.' This suggests a desire to bring the violence under the army's control and direction, not to reduce the ferocity and scale of the anti-communist killings.[60] Variations in the timing and scale of the violence across the disparate parts of the archipelago do not simply reflect variations in the depth of anti-communist feeling; the exclusion of West Java was derived from pragmatic concerns about the threat from regionalist movements, and the relatively delayed start of systematic mass killing in Bali is attributable to the late arrival of the army on that island – so the variations reflect, in the words of Kenneth R. Young, 'the variable speeds at which [different elements of the Indonesian population] have been ... integrated into the nation.'[61]

Indeed, the timing of the slaughter in Bali offers perhaps the most convincing refutation of the pervasive myth that the killings were a spontaneous response to the 30th September affair. Noting that the systematic mass slaughter on the islands did not begin until the arrival of Java-based military forces, Robert Cribb concludes that 'a number of stories make it clear that it was the arrival of army units with death lists which played a key role in prompting the killings'.[62] Once the systematic killing started, the scale and efficiency of the slaughter was so great that it would surely have assuaged the concerns about leniency expressed by the PNI in October. Geoffrey Robinson has suggested that the intense enthusiasm shown by the local military commanders may have been, to a certain extent, attributable to a desire to deflect attention from the fact that the 30th September Movement had received some support within their circle, and allay suspicions as to where their loyalties rested.[63] The devastating scale of the slaughter – an estimated six thousand people were killed in just three days in December, with eyewitness accounts reporting that corpses were dumped into the sea or in mass graves – could not have been achieved without critical logistical support from the army, in the form of weapons, ammunition, trucks, communications and detention centres. Trucks were loaded with alleged communists, and unloaded at a warehouse. The victims, hands bound, were shot, one by one, with automatic weapons.[64] The executions usually took place either within military encampments, or in hamlets with a solid base of PNI/NU support. The brief account of the historian of the Jembrana district, I Wayan Reken, provides a succinct appraisal of the violence in that district:

> 'Through the month of December, the Army with angry people of the Front Pancasila destroyed the communists in the most horrible massacre. It was a river of blood in which several thousands were killed in Jembrana alone, a tragic summary of the history of Jembrana.'[65]

Once the army had begun their operations, the PNI mobilised local paramilitary groups, who embarked on a systematic programme of killing, moving from village to village using lists of party members or denunciations by local informers.[66] A visiting Dutch journalist, Paul van't Veer, described how the killers would enter villages, round up the communists and take them by truck to another village, where they were either slaughtered with knives or shot dead in police prisons. Victims' extended families were usually also killed, to mitigate against the possibility of any later acts of revenge.[67] On occasions, the army would hand back to a village the communists it had captured, and order the people of the village to kill them themselves – the villagers would have little option but to club and knife the communists to death.[68] There were numerous rapes of women accused of being members of the PKI-affiliated *Gerwani* women's group. A PNI leader from Negara named Wadagda, who was a younger brother of a leading PNI figure named Wedestra Suyasa, raped tens of women who had been accused of being PKI members. While the overwhelming majority of such attacks went totally unpunished, Wedastra Suyasa was brought before a court and criminally prosecuted in March 1967. He was sentence to three years in gaol.[69] Long-standing cultural traditions of community obligation and deference to authority served to facilitate the process, as illustrated in the case of the group of young boys who, when asked why they had killed three PKI members near the Pura Besakih temple, offered the following simple explanation: 'Some authorities just came by one day and said to get rid of them ... so we did.'[70]

Mutilation features prominently in accounts of the killings on Bali. One account tells of a *bupati* (district head) who was detained by the military and executed in custody. Later the same day, one of the soldiers involved in the execution was seen with a paper parcel containing his ears and fingers.[71] Don Moser describes how one Balinese mutilated his friend before killing him: 'Ali took his *parang* – a short swordlike knife used for chopping in the fields – and cut off his friend's left ear, then his right ear, then his nose. Finally he raised his *parang* high and chopped his head off.'[72] This tendency has been attributed to religious beliefs, in particular the belief that an imperfect corpse will not acquire heavenly status and will therefore be unable to wreak revenge upon the killer, a notion echoed in the allegation that the killers on Bali put whitewash into their victims' eyes so that 'the eyes would not take their picture into the other world'.[73] More mundane explanations are equally convincing, however: there is little to suggest that the violent dismemberment of victims was motivated by anything more than the wanton savagery that is not peculiar to any religion or culture and perhaps, in some instances, a more pragmatic desire to minimise the risk of revenge attacks by mutilating the victim's body beyond recognition. In some instances, mutilation would be carried out for symbolic purposes that were more political than religious, as in the case of the Suteja's former associate I Gde Puger, whose excessive corpulence had been widely attributed to his notorious corruption and who was, accordingly, made to endure the cruelty of having pieces of flesh sliced from his body while he was still alive, before eventually being killed.[74]

As elsewhere in Indonesia, the killing in Bali was underpinned by a rhetoric of cultural and religious symbolism. The Hindu leader Ida Bagus set the tone in early October when he declared that the communists were 'the cruellest enemies of religion, and must be eliminated and destroyed down to the roots'.[75] The killers also exploited the religious beliefs of their victims in order that they might go more compliantly to their deaths; victims would be offered the opportunity to choose *nyupat* – a Balinese concept of willing death incorporating repentance which guarantees against a hellish afterlife – and being shot. Those who chose *nyupat* died in exactly the same way as the others, just in a different spot. Few received proper burial rites or a customary cremation.[76] As Geoffrey Robinson points out, the PKI was not self-evidently atheistic, nor was it responsible for Bali's economic and social problems; the perception of the PKI as a pernicious, uncompromisingly atheistic force was something that had to be nourished. Likewise the idea that Indonesia suffered from some sort of cosmic imbalance or impurity, which needed to be rectified by mass murder, had no basis in the precepts of Balinese Hinduism, but originated with the Indonesian military leadership.[77] This construct was none the less accepted wholesale by influential commentators such as John Hughes, whose book *Indonesian Upheaval* – discussed further below – has achieved an influence in this field out of all proportion to its merits.

Two conceptions of the killings: Oriental madness versus systematic massacre

It is surprisingly difficult to find, in the literature on the Indonesian killings of 1965-66, an analysis of the killings that is entirely devoid of Orientalist nonsense. Geoffrey Robinson's assessment of the killings, devised in relation to the Bali killings but equally applicable to the massacre as a whole, comes close. He insists that the slaughter was not simply the result of a political vacuum in which antagonistic forces ran wild: 'Elements of the state itself – especially local and national military commands – in alliance with powerful civilian political forces and with the support of international actors, consciously sanctioned and encouraged the annihilation of a substantial segment of the population.'[78] A considerable proportion of contemporary and more recent commentary on the killings has, however, placed a heavy emphasis on the role of Oriental mysticism and tradition in the events of 1965-66. It is worth reviewing the various ways in which Orientalist clichés have been employed to explain the killings, if only because they have had such a pervasive influence in the literature pertaining to this subject – the main title of Robinson's own study, *Dark Side of Paradise*, would appear to be a minor concession to this approach – and because they have served to obfuscate and distort the truth of the killings. The clichés tend towards a conception of the killings as a spontaneous, spiritually-driven popular effort to cleanse the archipelago of a resented impurity. This approach has the effect of exculpating the Suharto-Nasution regime and its foreign backers (see Chapters Three and Four, below) by presenting the mass slaughter as the product of a sort of primitive Eastern madness infused with witchcraft, providence and other supernatural phenomena, which was nonetheless triggered by a reaction of 'forces' that had something of the inevitability and certainty of the natural sciences. As we shall see, this conception has little or no basis in fact, and the more prosaic reality was of a systematic killing comparable to the twentieth century's other major holocausts.

John Hughes was one of only a small handful of Western journalists in Indonesia at the time of the killings. His account – the first detailed account of the slaughter to be read in the West – was published under the title *Indonesian Upheaval* in 1967, and later re-published as *The End of Sukarno: A Coup That Misfired: A Purge that Ran Wild* in 2002. In a brazenly one-sided account, Hughes – who would go on to work for the US State Department – concluded that the killings were 'fortunate for Indonesia'[79], a necessary step to pre-empt an otherwise inevitable communist takeover.[80] Hughes drew a comparison with the conscious and deliberate suicidal violence of Balinese fighters in the face of Dutch guns in 1906, concluding that Indonesia in 1965-66 was permeated by that same sense of a 'mass joyful death-wish'[81] which he believed characterised the heroic self-sacrificing violence of an earlier era. Hughes was by no means alone in this view – the *New York Times* journalist CL Sulzberger attributed the killings to a 'strange Malay streak, that inner frenzied blood-lust which has given to other languages one of their few Malay words: *amok*.'[82] Robert Shaplen of the *New Yorker* magazine insisted that 'the rest of the rational world' should not judge the Indonesians, as they 'were able to explain the bloodbath, at least to their own satisfaction, in ancient terms of catharsis and the eradication of evil.' The people were 'emotionally and psychologically ready to run amok.'[83] As Robert Cribb has pointed out, the 'running *amok*' concept has been totally misappropriated in this context: the concept, as traditionally understood, involves the redemption of honour by means of frenzied violence (either by an individual in personal or financial difficulties, or by a group of soldiers in an unwinnable military situation) resulting in the death of the amokker.[84] The massacres of 1965-66 were certainly not characterised by that sense of pathetic desperation on the part of the killers which defines what it means to 'run *amok*'. A superficial level of research would have established that the Indonesian army and the Muslim and nationalist youths, who together perpetrated the massacre, could not truly be said to have been 'running *amok*'; the phrase sounds good, however, and has the ring of anthropological insight, and accordingly it appears frequently in both journalistic and – mercifully to a slightly lesser extent – academic accounts of the killings. Sparse accounts of victims going to their deaths in ceremonial robes, with an air of defeated resignation about them, have been transposed in the commentary into an all-encompassing vision of collective suicide (the 'mass joyful death-wish'), replete with ceremonial trimmings. As Robinson points out, this description does not square with the historical evidence – the vast majority of victims did not dress in ceremonial costume, but were transported to execution centres in the middle of the night, and unceremoniously killed, often after being badly mutilated. Many PKI members put up a fight, and others fled or hid.[85] The assumption that those who did face death with resignation did so out of a sense of religious fatalism or guilt (rather than a rational realisation that resistance was futile) falls squarely within that category of racist thought which ascribes to Eastern individuals a presumption that their motivation for action is religious or spiritual rather than rational, informing a conception of the Oriental as an unthinking automaton or drone. Such inaccuracies form part of a wider blanket of obscurantism which can perhaps best be explained by the personal political sympathies of contemporary commentators, at a point in history when the struggle against world communism was a primary concern for most mainstream commentators, and indeed took priority over factual accuracy in reporting; old-fashioned racism probably also played an important part. Whatever the exact proportions, respectively, of deliberate, politically-motivated obfuscation and politically-neutral racist cultural and anthropological stereotyping, it is difficult to overlook the wild, other-worldly indulgence of Don Moser's assessment of what he calls an 'orgy of cruelty [driven by] mass hysteria': 'Nowhere but on these weird and lovely islands ... could affairs have erupted so unpredictably, so violently, tinged not only with fanaticism but with blood-lust and something like witchcraft.' Sulzberger's observation that the killings took place in 'violent Asia, where life is cheap', accord with this general tendency to construct a different moral framework in which the killings can be received with rather less horror than comparable events in the Western world, because this is 'violent Asia', where people 'run *amok*', where this sort of thing just happens from time to time. Barely two decades after the horrors of European fascism, Sulzberger's implicit comment on the relative value of human life in Western countries appears at best somewhat complacent, at worst extremely naïve.

As well as explaining the killings themselves, Indonesia's cultural idiosyncrasies were cited to explain the long-standing antagonisms which provided the context for the massacres. In inciting the peasantry to act assertively to effect the enforcement of land reform laws, the PKI was pursuing an agenda which ran contrary to long-established traditional Indonesian cultural notions of passivity and conservatism among the peasantry. Guy Pauker, of the Washington think-tank the RAND Corporation, observed that the 'local custom' in Java was to 'do all things quietly, subtly, politely and communally – even starve.'[86] By inciting the peasantry to improve their lot, the communists were attacking 'local custom'. Elaborating on this theme, the former US ambassador to Indonesia, Marshall Green, attributed the ferocity of the anti-communist violence to the fact that 'communism, with its atheism and talk of class warfare, was abhorrent to the way of life of rural Indonesia, especially in Java and Bali, whose cultures place great strength on tolerance, harmony, mutual assistance ...'[87] While there is some truth in the claim that the PKI's socialist politics and assertive campaigning methods upset the balance in Indonesian rural life, it is more helpful to conceive of their impact in terms of political and economic power relations – viz. a threat to the traditional landowning elite – than in terms of an abstract, generic cultural-religious equilibrium. The violent history of civil war in Java in the 17th and 18th centuries belies any tradition of harmony. In any event, the mutual antagonisms between the PKI on the one hand, and the conservative (Muslim and nationalist) elements on the other, were not sufficient to explain the systematic nature and the massive scale of the violence. The notion that a traditionally passive and indifferent people could suddenly be stirred to frenzied murderous violence in defence of 'tolerance, harmony, [and] mutual assistance' proposes a logical leap that does not quite withstand close scrutiny; perhaps the employment of clichés about sudden Oriental madness constitutes an attempt to bridge this logical gap.

The mundane truth of the matter is succinctly summarised by Kenneth R. Young, who concludes that the killing was 'more than the climax of years of internal struggle within Indonesian society. It was a political choice deliberately taken by the military commanders who controlled perhaps the only instrument of State policy that could be relied upon – the army itself.'[88] In short, however great the tensions were between the PKI and the nationalist and religious elements, were it not for the deliberate and planned actions of the Indonesian army, they would certainly not have led to a large-scale systematic massacre of somewhere between 500,000 and one million people between October 1965 and April 1966. Although the causes of the hostility towards the PKI were unquestionably political, it is important to bear in mind that the party had not been pursuing a revolutionary policy at any point in its rise to prominence in the 1950s and 1960s. The party's activities were confined to legitimate parliamentary campaigning and small-scale 'actions' aimed at encouraging the enforcement of land reform laws passed by the central government in Jakarta. Harold Crouch's summary identifies conservative opposition to the party's essentially reformist programme as the true basis of anti-PKI hostility:

> The party's mass base among the peasantry had been attracted by the PKI's vigour in defending the interests of the *abangan* (nominally Islamic) poor, which conflicted with those of the better-off peasantry and the Muslim community, but the party's program had been in no way 'revolutionary'.[89]

Even in the brutal and bloody history of the Twentieth Century, examples of government-led mass murder, on a comparable scale, against a domestic population are relatively rare. A mere two decades after the horrors of the Second World War, the most powerful and influential nations in the Western world tended to present themselves, in everything from their political rhetoric to their cultural output, as being fundamentally ideologically opposed to the sort of vicious barbarism that the Indonesian army was inflicting upon its own population. On this occasion, however, the governments of both the United States and Great Britain, senior and junior partners respectively in the leadership of the 'free world' against global communism, expressed great satisfaction at the scale and efficiency of the slaughter, and even took steps, where conveniently possible, to assist the Indonesian army and the nascent Suharto regime. It is to this matter that we now turn.

Notes
1 *Angkatan Bersendjata* editorial, 14th October 1965, cited in Geoffrey Robinson, *The Dark Side of Paradise: Political Violence in Bali* (New York: Cornell University Press, 1995), p281 (footnote).
2 Robinson, *Dark Side of Paradise*, pp285-286.
3 Robert Cribb, 'Problems in the Historiography of the Killings in Indonesia' in Robert Cribb Ed, *The Indonesian Killings of 1965-66* (Clayton: Monash University Centre for Southeast Asian Studies, 1990), p29, citing Roger Paget, 'The Indonesian Military and the Burden of Power' *Pacific Affairs*, Vol. XL, Nos. 3 & 4, Fall & Winter, 1967/8 , pp295-296.
4 Cited in John Hughes, *The End of Sukarno: A Coup That Misfired: A Purge that Ran Wild* (Singapore: Archipelago Press, 2002)
5 Hughes, *The End of Sukarno*, p201.
6 Sukarno would not be formally displaced as head of state for another eighteen months. The nature of Suharto's new regime is discussed in Chapter Five.
7 Crouch, *Army and Politics*, pp141-142.
8 A detailed examination of the 30th September operations in Central Java appears in Crouch, *Army and Politics*, Chapter 5.
9 Cited in Dinas Sejarah & Angkatan Darat, 'Crushing the G30S/PKI in Central Java', in Cribb, *Indonesian Killings*, p164.
10 Hughes, *The End of Sukarno*, pp201-202.
11 Hughes, *The End of Sukarno*, pp162-163.
12 Hughes, *The End of Sukarno*, p169.
13 Stanley Karnow, 'First Report on Horror in Indonesia', *Washington Post*, 17th April 1966, cited in Roosa, *Pretext for Mass Murder*, pp25-26.

14 Anderson & McVey, *A Preliminary Analysis of the October 1, 1965 Coup in Indonesia* (Ithaca, New York: Cornell Unversity SE Asia Program, 1971) p63, cited in Roosa, *Pretext for Mass Murder*, p22. Authors' italics.
15 Simon, *Broken Triangle*, p125.
16 NCNA 30th January 1967, cited in Simon, *Broken Triangle*, pp143-144.
17 Jakarta Domestic Service, 17th May 1967, cited in *Broken Triangle*, p161
18 Roosa, *Pretext for Mass Murder*, p22.
19 Suharto, *My Thoughts, Words, and Deeds: An Autobiography* (Jakarta: Citra Lamtoro Gung Persada, 1991), p114, cited in Roosa, *Pretext for Mass Murder*, p23.
20 Cited in Roosa, *Pretext for Mass Murder*, p22.
21 Theodore Friend, *Indonesian Destinies* (Massachusetts: Harvard University Press, 2003) p109, citing Yasir's accounts
22 Bu Yeti, 'Survival: Bu Yeti's Story', in Cribb, *Indonesian Killings*, 231.
23 Robert Cribb and Colin Brown, *Modern Indonesia: A History Since 1945* (New York: Longman, 1995), p103.
24 Kenneth R. Young, 'Local and National Influences in the Violence of 1965' in Cribb, *Indonesian Killings*, pp63-99.
25 Ibid, pp72-73.
26 Ibid, p74.
27 Ibid, pp75-76.
28 Ibid, p71.
29 Ibid, p79.
30 Ibid, pp79-80.
31 Ibid, p83.
32 Ibid, p84.
33 Anonymous, 'Additional Data on Counter-Revolutionary Cruelty in Indonesia, especially in East Java', in Cribb, *Indonesian Killings*, pp169-176. There do not appear to be any substantial doubts as to the credibility of these accounts. In particular, some of the accounts indicate a detailed level of local knowledge to which any outsider would have had little access. In view of the considerable personal risk involved for both the researchers and the subjects, it is unlikely that these accounts are fabricated.
34 'Additional Data on Counter-Revolutionary Cruelty in Indonesia', p170 published in the Jakarta Press on a number of occasions in 1980, 1983, and 1985.
35 Ibid, p171.
36 Ibid, p171.
37 Ibid, p172.
38 Ibid, p172.
39 Ibid, p172.
40 Ibid, p173.
41 Ibid, p175.
42 Hughes, *The End of Sukarno*, p170.

43 Hughes, *The End of Sukarno*, p172.
44 Seymour Topping, 'Slaughter of Reds Gives Indonesia a Grim Legacy', *New York Times*, 24th August 1966, cited in Roosa, *Pretext for Mass Murder*, p26.
45 Friend, *Indonesian Destinies*, pp109-110, citing the personal account of Norma Zecha.
46 Sukarno's speech, 17th December 1965, cited in Crouch, *Army and Politics*, p157.
47 *Suara* (daily newspaper) 9th December 1965, cited in Geoffrey Robinson, *The Dark Side of Paradise: Political Violence in Bali* (London: Cornell University Press, 1995), 298.
48 Centre for Village Studies, Gadjah Mada University, 'Rural Violence in Bali', in Cribb, *Indonesian Killings*, p243.
49 Robinson, *Dark Side of Paradise*, p287.
50 *Suara* 29th October 1965, cited in Robinson, *Dark Side of Paradise*, p288.
51 *Suara Indonesia* (Denpasar daily), 29th October 1965, cited in Robinson, *Dark Side of Paradise*, p289.
52 Cited in Robinson, *Dark Side of Paradise*, p290.
53 *Suara* (Denpasar) 5th November 1965, cited in Robinson, *Dark Side of Paradise*, p293
54 *Suara* (Denpasar) 21st November 1965, cited in Robinson, *Dark Side of Paradise*, p293.
55 *Suara* (Denpasar) 18th November 1965, cited in Robinson, *Dark Side of Paradise*, pp293-294.
56 *Suara* (Denpasar) 1st December 1965, cited in Robinson, *Dark Side of Paradise*, p294.
57 *Suara* (Denpasar) 1st December 1965, cited in Robinson, *Dark Side of Paradise*, p294.
58 Soe Hok Gie, 'The Mass Killing in Bali', in Cribb, *Indonesian Killings*, p255.
59 Most notably Hughes, *The End of Sukarno*, p190. According to Hughes' account, the bulk of the slaughter was carried out prior to the army's arrival on the island – 'With the arrival of the para-commandos, the worst was over'.
60 Robinson, *Dark Side of Paradise*, pp293-297, citing the translation of the original interview transcript in Dharmawan Tjonronegoro, *Ledakan Fitnah Subversi G-30-S* (Jakarta: Matoa, 1966).
61 Young, 'Local and National Influences in the Violence of 1965', p96.
62 Robert Cribb, 'Bali', in Cribb, *Indonesian Killings*, p247.
63 Robinson, *Dark Side of Paradise*, p293.
64 Robinson, *Dark Side of Paradise*, pp297-298, citing anonymous eyewitness account, 4th October 1986.
65 Robinson, *Dark Side of Paradise*, p298, citing I Wayan Rken, 'A History of Djembrana form the 18th Century', Manuscript.
66 Young, 'Local and National Influences in the Violence of 1965', p92.

67 Paul van't Veer, 'Bali zuivert zich zelf na gruwelijke moordgolf', *Vrij Uit*, 17 Dec 1966, cited in Robinson, *Dark Side of Paradise*, p298.
68 Hughes, *The End of Sukarno*, p189.
69 Soe Hok Gie, 'The Mass Killing in Bali', p256.
70 Don Moser, 'Where the Rivers Ran Crimson from Butchery', *Life*, 1st July 1966, cited in Robinson, *Dark Side of Paradise*, p299
71 Ibid.
72 Ibid.
73 John Gittings, 'The Black Hole of Bali', *Guardian Weekly* 23 Sep 1990, cited in Robert Cribb, 'Problems in the Historiography of the Killings in Indonesia', p30.
74 Cribb, 'Problems in the Historiography of the Killings in Indonesia', p30, citing Horace Sutton, 'Indonesia's Night of Terror', *Saturday Review* 4th February 1967, p27.
75 *Suara* (Denpasar) 7th October 1965, cited in Robinson, *Dark Side of Paradise*, p300.
76 Robinson, *Dark Side of Paradise*, p301.
77 Ibid, pp301-302.
78 Ibid, p303.
79 Hughes, *The End of Sukarno*, p173.
80 Ibid, p199.
81 Hughes, *The End of Sukarno*, pp190-191. Hughes' account is replete with this type of insight. Attributing the mass slaughter to the communists' disruption of 'an island in a state of perpetual enchantment with its own mystique', Hughes asserts that many victims went willingly to their deaths: '[Bali's communists] had seen the mistake of their Communist affiliation and by dying would be helping cleanse both themselves and the island', citing as his source the undocumented accounts of unnamed 'Balinese intellectuals'.
82 Cyrus Sulzberger, 'Foreign Affairs: When a Nation Runs Amok', *New York Times*, 14th April 1966, cited in Roosa, *Pretext for Mass Murder*, p27.
83 Shaplen, *Time out of Hand: Revolution and Reaction in Southeast Asia* (New York: Harper and Row, 1969) p128, cited in Roosa, *Pretext for Mass Murder*, pp27-28.
84 Robert Cribb, 'Problems in the Historiography of the Killings in Indonesia', p33, citing John C. Spires, *Running Amok: An Historical Inquiry* (Athens, Ohio: Ohio Univeristy Center for International Studies, 1988).
85 Robinson, *Dark Side of Paradise*, pp279-280.
86 Guy Pauker, 'Political Consequences of Rural Development Programs in Indonesia', *Pacific Affairs* 41 (Fall 1968), p390, cited in Robinson, *Dark Side of Paradise*, p276.
87 Cited in Robinson, *Dark Side of Paradise*, p277.
88 Young, 'Local and National Influences in the Violence of 1965', p86.
89 Crouch, *Army and Politics*, pp155-156.

CHAPTER THREE

'A Model Destabilisation Plan'

The United States and Suharto's Rise to Power

For the United States in this period, the politics of the developing world was viewed at all times through the prism of Cold War policy, and Indonesia was no exception. Foreign policy considerations were informed – indeed, to a great extent, dictated – by the so-called 'domino theory', which posited that the collapse of one Asian country to communism would inevitably lead to the collapse of its neighbour and so on until, eventually, the whole of Central and East Asia had fallen within the orbit of communism. It was on the basis of this fear that the United States justified a series of interventions after the Second World War, including the covert overthrow of reformist regimes in Iran (1953) and Guatemala (1954), and the overt military action in Vietnam (which was begun in 1959 and was becoming increasingly problematic for the United States by 1965). At the far end of the imaginary 'row' of dominos stood Indonesia, arguably the biggest 'domino' of the lot, with its important strategic location and its great demographic weight (Indonesia had the fifth-largest population in the world) and geographical expanse, as well as its abundance of natural resources. It was especially important as a source of oil, tin and rubber, with potential for further exploitation of gold, silver and nickel – it was certainly a far richer country, in these terms, than the nation of Vietnam, for whose 'protection' from communism the US was to spend over a decade engaged in military combat. For the United States, it was essential that Indonesia be kept within the capitalist world, preferably as a trading partner of Japan, in order to facilitate the economic progress of the latter and secure her against assimilation by Chinese or Russian communism. As early as December 1954, the National Security Council determined that the United States should use 'all feasible covert means', including 'armed force if necessary', to prevent the richest parts of Indonesia falling into communist hands.[1] By late 1957, the Eisenhower administration had come to the conclusion that the most effective way to counter the meteoric rise of the PKI would be to break up the archipelago into smaller units.² With these considerations in mind, the CIA provided arms and supplies to the local Muslim rebels who proclaimed a new, revolutionary government in the archipelago's richest island, Sumatra, in February 1958.

1959 – 1965: A Change of Policy

The failure of the Permesta uprising, and the subsequent hardening of anti-American sentiment among nationalists and the military, caused the US to re-think its strategy. Recognising that hostility towards the Indonesian national army would be counter-productive, and noting, in particular, that the officers who had played the leading role in suppressing the rebellion (Nasution and Yani) were staunch anti-communists, Washington changed tack. A National Security Council Special Report of January 1959 identified the army as the 'principle obstacle to the continued growth of Communist strength', and predicted that civilian non-communists 'could, with the backing of the Army, turn the tide against the Communist party in the political field'.³ Instead of seeking conflict with the Indonesian military by supporting regionalist rebellions, the US would now seek to co-opt the Indonesian military by providing US-based training for Indonesian officers, donating and selling weapons, and providing substantial financial aid. From 1958 to 1965, the US spent an annual sum of between $10million and $20million on military assistance to Indonesia.⁴ During this period, in the words of John Roosa, 'the consistent US strategy … was to help the army officers prepare themselves for a violent attack upon the PKI.'⁵ The new policy included an extensive training programme for Indonesian officers in army schools in the US such as those at Fort Bragg and Fort Leavenworth. While 2,800 Indonesian officers were brought to the US for training between 1950 and 1965, the majority of these arrived in the period after 1958.⁶ In a direct attempt to compete with the grass-roots work that was winning the PKI so much popular support, the US promoted a 'civic action' programme, whereby army-backed civilian front organisations would get involved with 'projects useful to [the] local population at all levels in such fields as education, training, public works, agriculture, transportation, communications, health, sanitation and others contributing to economic and social development, which should also serve to improve the standing of the military forces with the population.'[7] This implied an enhanced role for the military in public life which accorded with Nasution's own, quasi-fascist vision of a corporatist military state, as well as the strategy proposed by an influential State Department Policy Planning Council, whose January 1963 report expressly recommended encouraging military takeovers in underdeveloped countries at the expense of civilian government.[8]

While military assistance received top priority, the US government sought to destabilise Indonesia by withholding economic aid; in his memoir, US Ambassador Howard Jones recalls the decision of President Johnson, in December 1963, to withhold economic aid which Kennedy would have supplied 'almost as a matter of routine'[9], thus helping to aggravate the country's desperate economic problems and foment unrest. Peter Dale Scott notes that this strongly suggests that 'US aggravation of Indonesia's economic woes in 1963-65 was a matter of policy rather than inadvertence.'[10] From 1963 onwards, Jones recalls, the 'US government undertook no new commitments of assistance' (as we shall see below, this claim is not quite accurate), but merely by maintaining their existing assistance to the Indonesian army and police, the US 'fortified them for a virtually inevitable showdown with the burgeoning PKI.'[11] While economic aid was cut off and US-Indonesian relations kept ostensibly frosty, military aid continued to flow. In Fiscal Year 1965, the number of personnel from the US Military Assistance Program in Jakarta actually increased, to an unprecedented high of thirty-two.[12] Peter Dale Scott is correct, therefore, in concluding that the US 'was not at arm's length from the ugly political developments of 1965', despite what government spokesmen and press reports might have claimed.[13] For the United States, relations with Indonesia during this period were conceived in terms of support for a 'state within a state' – comprising the army and police force, with which the US was actively cultivating a strong relationship – alongside open hostility to the official Indonesian state as represented by Sukarno. When full-scale violence began in October 1965, the 'civic action groups', set up with US funding and training, would be at the centre of the organisational structure which implemented the killings. By the summer of 1965, the Indonesian military were quietly confident of their strength. Lieutenant General Yani assured the US military attaché, George Benson, that he was not worried about the PKI's apparent political ascendancy: 'We have the guns,' he said, 'and we have kept guns out of their hands. So if there's a clash, we'll wipe them out'.[14]

October 1965: The Killing Begins

The records of US foreign policy officials' deliberations and discussions in relation to the events of 1965-66 are, for the most part, declassified and publicly available in the State Department's *Foreign Relations of the United States* series. Although a significant proportion of the records remain classified to this day, the declassified documentation provides a valuable insight into how senior US policymakers approached the crisis as it unfolded. A central figure was US Ambassador Marshall Green who, in May 1965, succeeded the long-serving Howard Jones – the latter had served in Indonesia for the entirety of the 1958-65 period prior to the 30th September affair, overseeing the cultivation of the United States' strong links with the Indonesian army on behalf of three different Washington administrations.

A CIA situation report transmitted in the early hours of 1st October 1965 reveals consternation at 'a power move which may have far-reaching implications'[15]. The report identifies the movement's chief purpose as 'the elimination of any political role by anti-communist Army elements.'[16] Events moved fast on 1st October, however, with Undersecretary of State George Ball advising his colleague Secretary of State Dean Rusk at 3.15pm that a 'counter coup' was already underway.[17] This 'counter-coup' was led by General Suharto. The most senior of the plotters' targets, General Nasution, had dramatically fled from the plotters on the night of 30th September. By 3.45pm it was clear that 'Nasution [had] taken back Djakarta radio station', with Ball expressing the hope that Nasution would 'keep going and clean up [the] PKI' – this would be 'the most optimistic expectation'.[18] Several months earlier, in March 1965, Ambassador Jones had told a closed-door meeting of State Department officials that such a development would not be unwelcome: 'From our viewpoint, of course, an unsuccessful coup attempt by the PKI might be the most effective development to start [a] reversal of political trends in Indonesia'. Jones believed that a coup would provide the 'clear-cut kind of challenge which would galvanize effective reaction'.[19]

By 2nd October, the 'coup' had utterly collapsed. The army strategic reserve, led by General Suharto, outmanoeuvred the rebel battalions and restored order in the capital. Details began to emerge that the PKI had aligned themselves with the Untung 'coup'. On 2nd October, the PKI's Jakarta daily *Harian Rakjat* published an editorial in praise of the Movement, which it depicted as an internal army affair. While the situation was 'still pretty opaque', the conversation between Ball and Rusk suggests a note of cautious optimism, particularly with regard to the fact that the 'PKI have definitely aligned themselves with Untung [30th September Movement] side which seems to be the losing side', and this 'could work out advantageously later in the day.'[20] From the very beginning of the crisis, therefore, it is clear that the position of the PKI was at the very forefront of the thinking of US decision-makers, despite the fact that it was by no means clear that the PKI was directly involved in the 'coup'. In fact, it is clear that Rusk understood the 30th September Movement to be an internal army affair, not a PKI-instigated 'coup', judging from his reference to the Movement as the 'Untung coup' and his surprise at the PKI's decision to come out in support of it. By 5th October, the Embassy in Jakarta was identifying ways in which the United States could 'help shape developments to our advantage'.[21] It was essential to 'avoid overt involvement', the Embassy stressed in its telegram to the Department of State, but contacts with Nasution and Suharto should be maintained, and extended if possible. The priority, however, the 'most needed immediate assistance' to the army, was to 'spread the story of [the] PKI's guilt, treachery and brutality', although this should be done in such a way that it should not be identifiable as 'solely or largely [a] US effort.'[22]

The PKI's treatment of the 'coup' as an internal army matter prompted fears among US staff that the opportunity to strike at the PKI might have passed. Ball expressed his concern that the army were 'losing a lot of critical time … because [the] PKI [has] disavowed [the] September 30 movement and are moving toward [a] position of respectability.' The State Department was anxious that the army, which had begun its operations against the PKI, should 'maintain momentum' and not be swayed by the 'political manipulations' of the embattled President Sukarno, who had sought to play down the 'coup' as an internal army matter, and was likely to urge restraint.[23] In order to maintain the propaganda assault against the PKI, it would not be necessary, for the time being at least, for US sources to fabricate stories – it was clear that the Indonesian press, and the army-run newspapers in particular, did not need assistance in this regard – but the Voice of America broadcaster would run an 'information programme' which would cite existing Indonesian sources 'pointing [the] finger at [the] PKI and playing up [the] brutality of [the] September 30 rebels'.[24]

As the army-led purge of the PKI continued, the State Department agonised over the tactical question of how it could influence events without offending the fervently nationalistic sensibilities of the Indonesian army and of Indonesian society at large. On the one hand, the US 'do not wish to give [the] army [the] impression that we are trying to inject ourselves into [the Indonesian] internal situation'; on the other hand, the army was probably hoping for positive gestures from the US, so that 'if [the] army's willingness to follow through against [the] PKI is in any way contingent on ... US, we do not wish [to] miss [the] opportunity [to consider] US action.'[25] For the time being, the Embassy and the State Department agreed, the US would 'move cautiously'.[26] As the army's position became more secure, the US became gradually more responsive to the Generals' request for logistical support, and on 14th October the Embassy approved a proposal to supply the Indonesian army with communications equipment – 'three Motorola P-31 hand-talkies ... with batteries and battery chargers' would be covertly supplied to the army via the military attaché immediately.[27] In the main, however, their approach with regard to 'further assistance of this kind' would remain cautious, and this 'small quiet gesture' should be understood merely 'in terms of helping a friend in need'.[28]

Although Indonesia was undergoing a tumultuous internal transformation, the upheaval would necessarily have to be couched in the rhetoric of nationalism and independence, which had been a central foundation of the Indonesian state. Despite a crumbling economy and the divisions caused by his close association with communist China, Sukarno remained a popular figure, and both the Indonesian army and their supporters in the State Department understood that it was necessary to at least pay lip service to Sukarno's fervently nationalistic rhetoric, which emphasised the need for vigilance against the encroachments of an external enemy – *NEKOLIM*, an acronym for neo-colonialists and imperialists – in defence of the independent Indonesia. The Embassy correctly predicted that, while the 'anti-NEKOLIM' posture would be retained by the army, 'the army may well seek to twist [the] definition of the term when this suits the army's purposes'.[29] The new regime would maintain an anti-imperialist stance, but the aggressor would be communist China, linked with the PKI, to whose treachery were attributed the murderous intrigues of the '30 September Movement'. Violent mob attacks against Chinese nationals and their property accompanied the anti-communist violence during this period, as the Chinese community in Indonesia – envied and resented for their superior economic position – were scapegoated by a media campaign which encouraged violence against them.

Although the State Department lagged behind events to an extent, the summary executions of rank-and-file PKI members were known to it at the very latest by 20th October, when the Embassy telegrammed to advise that 'Some thousand of PKI cadres have reportedly been arrested in [the] Djakarta area alone and several hundred of them have been executed.'[30] Ambassador Green expressed some anxiety over whether the anti-PKI campaign would extend fully to a campaign against 'communism as such ... including associations with China and other bloc countries', but for the time being he was certainly satisfied that the army 'has ... been working hard at destroying [the] PKI', adding a note of personal approval: 'I, for one, have increasing respect for its determination and organization in carrying out this crucial assignment.'[31] The army-led massacre took an estimated death toll of 500,000 victims, who were selected on the basis of actual or alleged links with the PKI. The link between the PKI and the 'coup' of 30th September was therefore central to the Indonesian army's justification of its massacre of the communists. A US Embassy telegram of 22nd October expressed considerable surprise that the PKI, which had been making steady and significant gains through a peaceful policy of cooperation with the Indonesian state under the leadership of DN Aidit, should have made on overt bid for power at this time, concluding that the 'Only tenable conclusion ... is that Aidit and [the] PKI were under heavy pressure from [China] to produce [an] abrupt and prompt victory ...'.[32] Subsequent research has shown that the most plausible explanation of the PKI's involvement in the 'coup' is that a small handful of PKI leaders decided, without consulting the party, to throw in the party's lot with the rebelling officers.[33] From the point of view of US Cold War objectives, however, the guilt or innocence of the hundreds of thousands who were murdered would appear to have been quite secondary to the strategic advantage gained by the elimination of the PKI as a political force in Indonesia. Having previously cut off economic aid to the country in 1963, exacerbating the economic problems which led to the country's unstable position in 1965, the US would now be 'disposed to help [the Indonesians]' to 'take rapid and effective steps to correct [the] current economic mess'.[34] In a memorandum to President Johnson, the National Security advisor McGeorge Bundy praised the army's 'considerable courage'.[35] As October drew to a close, Secretary of State Rusk advised the Embassy that 'The next few days, weeks or months may offer unprecedented opportunities for us to ... influence people and events.'[36] The State Department Assistant for Indonesia, DE Nuechterlein, confirmed that the Indonesian army was, on the whole, sufficiently well-equipped to 'deal effectively with [the PKI]', but the US should seek to supply 'small quantities of specific items which are in short supply or in a poor state of repair', advising that such items should be supplied 'through a third country, such as Thailand or Philippines', to ensure 'minimum risk of exposure', rather than reverting to an overt resumption of aid by way of an explicit Mutual Assistance Program.[37]

Concerns about army leniency appear to have abated by early November, with the Embassy reporting that 'Nasution ... is moving relentlessly to exterminate [the] PKI', and considering providing the army with 'small arms stocks ... of non-US origin, which could be obtained without any overt US Government involvement.'[38] While sympathetic towards the army's mass killing of communists and communist sympathisers, American diplomatic officials remained apprehensive about the likely nationalist orientation of the Suharto-Nasution regime. The Director of the Office of Southeast Pacific Affairs, David Cuthell, noted the army's opposition to the ongoing US involvement in Vietnam, and expressed fears that the army's 'strongly nationalistic ... economic orientation' might compromise the position of the US oil companies Stanvac and Caltex.[39] Reminding his colleague that the situation nonetheless constituted a remarkable shift from the position barely three months ago, when the PKI were in the ascendancy and the Indonesian 'domino' looked set to fall, he concluded on an optimistic note, noting that the new Indonesian stance was 'the best we can hope for', and that the army leadership in any case remained 'hostile in many respects to ... the Soviet Union [and] Communist China'.[40]

US officials were under no illusions about the expansive nature of the anti-communist purge. This operation was certainly not a question merely of decapitating the communist 'monster' by removing the higher and middle strata of the organisation. Reporting back to the State Department on 4th November, the Embassy confirmed that even 'Smaller fry [were] being systematically arrested and jailed or executed.'[41] At this point, General Sukendro was visiting Thailand and requesting arms assistance from the US via its Thai client. The Embassy in Rangoon telegrammed the State Department to ask for 'more explicit guidance' on how to handle the request for 'communications equipment and small arms to arm Moslem and nationalist youths in Central Java for use against the PKI'.[42] In an internal memorandum, the CIA acknowledged the difficulties posed by the question of provision of assistance to 'a group which cannot be considered a legal government nor yet a regime of proven reliability or longevity', concluding that the regime's 'legal authority as well as its de facto control must be confirmed' before overt assistance could be offered.[43] In the meantime, the US should not be 'too hesitant about the propriety of extending ... assistance provided we can do so covertly, in a manner which will not embarrass them or embarrass our government'.[44]

Whilst the US did not wish to be associated with overt support for the nascent Suharto regime and its total disregard for the rule of law and human rights, it was equally important for the longevity of the Suharto regime that the latter should not be perceived by the Indonesian people as a puppet of US imperial designs on the country. In an intriguing paragraph of which several lines remain classified, the report acknowledges the existence of mechanisms for the provision of 'covert credits for purchases deliver[ing] any of the types of the materiel requested to date in reasonable quantities'.[45] It is unlikely the full extent of US support for Suharto's campaign will be known as long as critical sections of the record remain classified. For the time being, the report concludes that requests for small arms and medicine should not be granted 'at this time', due to the danger of 'incurring political risk'. However, these risks should be 'weighed against the greater risks that failure to provide such aid' would incur. Accordingly, the avenues for 'covert implementation' through 'transmittal of funds … or delivery of the requested items … in discreet fashion', remained open, provided the generals could 'justify their needs in detail'.[46] On 11th November, the Embassy in Rangoon recommended the 'covert procurement of commercially available stock items' in response to to an 'urgent' request from General Sukendro for communications equipment to facilitate communications between military units in the Jakarta area.[47]

Gradually, further details emerged about the nature of the violence. The US Consulate in Medan reported to the State Department that officials from the nationalist youth organisation Pemuda Pantjasila promised to 'Kill every PKI member they can catch' and 'ignore public calls for calm'. Local Muslim leaders were treating the campaign as a 'holy war', and 'much indiscriminate killing is taking place', 'something like [a] real reign of terror', which was 'not discriminating … between PKI leaders and ordinary PKI members with no ideological bond to the party'.[48] The very next day, a National Security Council memorandum considered the 'urgent' need to provide communications equipment to the army to support this campaign, proposing such support be 'given' to the generals free of charge, in view of the army's difficult financial situation.[49] Noting the need for 'extreme care … in all aspects of this operation', the memorandum cites the 'security and personal safety of the leading anti-Communist leaders' as justification for the granting of covert aid.[50]

As November drew to a close, the CIA's assessment of the situation concluded that the Generals were 'engaged in a power struggle, not an ideological struggle, with [the PKI]'. The fact that a number of Indonesian army officers 'consider themselves to be Marxist socialists' was immaterial – the PKI was being eliminated principally because it was 'a rival for power within Indonesia'.[51] United States support was not limited to logistical support for the military. In November, the Embassy reported to the State Department recommending the release of fifty million rupiahs to fund the 'Kap-Gestapu movement', an army front organisation charged with organising the civilian involvement in the campaign against the PKI. Its activities had been an 'important factor in the army's program, and ... highly successful', and Ambassador Green was certain that there was 'no doubt whatsoever that Kap-Gestapu's activity is fully consonant with and coordinated by the army.' Green assured the State Department that the 'chances of detection' were 'as minimal as any black bag operation can be'.[52]

As the State Department was well aware, however, the Indonesian question would not be solved by force alone. With the Indonesian economy in a state of desperate disrepair – inflation had reached 134% by 1964, prior to the outbreak of the current crisis – the legitimacy of the new regime would hinge on whether it could halt and reverse an increasingly worrying rice shortage that threatened unpredictable political consequences. With this in mind, the Director of the Far East Region, FJ Blouin, advised that 'assistance to help the Indonesian Army consolidate its position should be granted promptly' if requested by the new regime. Such assistance should be treated as 'short-term aid ... [and] considered separately from long-term economic assistance', and as such it should be given 'without strings' – i.e. without any insistence upon assurances with respect to the position of US oil firms in Indonesia or with respect to the situation in Malaysia (discussed in Chapter Four).[53] By mid-December, the State Department had gathered, quite accurately, that the 'campaign to destroy [the] PKI is moving fairly swiftly and smoothly', and that a new government could even be in place 'within weeks', achieving 'the situation we have hoped for'.[54] By Christmas time, the Embassy could confidently report that the 'PKI is no longer a significant political force, and [the] Djakarta-Peking axis is in tatters'. There had been some diminution in the violence against the Chinese, but 'attacks on [the] tattered remnants of [the] PKI are being allowed to continue.'[55] Despite their optimism, US planners remained reluctant to provide overt military aid, citing concerns about how such assistance might be interpreted within Indonesia, and about the new regime's possible approach towards US economic assets in Indonesia and Southeast Asia at large. In any case, the efficiency of the anti-communist operation seemed to suggest that 'no US military assistance appears [to be] required for internal security ... at this time.'[56] The very generous assistance granted in the years prior to 1965 was bearing positive rewards with respect to 'internal security' – the economic situation was the area of greatest uncertainty.

In mid-January, US planners deliberated at some length over a request from the new Indonesian regime for around 350,000 tons of rice, 50 million yards of cotton cloth, and medical supplies, all amounting to an estimated cost of $50 million, by way of emergency assistance to help protect the new regime from the instability threatened by the economic crisis. The State Department emphasised concerns that 'Indonesia has not yet created [a] situation in which the US can be of assistance to Indonesia'. Noting that the elimination of the PKI had precipitated significant domestic economic reforms in a liberalising direction favoured by Washington, the Embassy expressed concerns that an improved economic situation could potentially induce complacency with respect to the pace of reform, so that economic assistance at this stage might actually 'retard [the] changes which Indonesia in its own interest must make'.[57] The request for economic assistance would be turned down for the time being. The central problem was the uncertainty regarding the status of Sukarno who, while still nominally head of state, was increasingly being marginalised as a significant political actor. Sukarno, who had attempted to dismiss the September 'coup' as merely 'a ripple in the ocean of the [Indonesian national] revolution', had made a number of defiant speeches in December in which he indicated an unwillingness to formally ban the PKI. Reviewing the situation in February, the Embassy concluded that the army 'may ... have rationalized that since Sukarno and his clique refused to cooperate willingly it might be [a] better tactic to leave them in power and let them bear full responsibility for [the] economic deterioration'. This was the path chosen by the Suharto-Nasution group, who considered that it would be more useful to retain Sukarno as a figurehead rather than incur unnecessary risks by trying to oust him at this stage. Sukarno would be slowly and quietly pushed out over an eighteen-month period, with Suharto only formally inaugurated as President in 1968. While the Embassy was still waiting for the particulars of the new situation to crystallise fully, Ambassador Green was pleased to advise, on 14th February 1966, of the 'favourable achievements' of the new regime, in particular that the communists in Indonesia 'have been decimated by wholesale massacre' and were unlikely to regroup effectively in any meaningful way.[58] A briefing note for President Johnson congratulated the new regime on 'employing brilliant "salami" tactics in eliminating the PKI', but warned that there were now 'two governments ... competing for power' – namely, the Sukarno faction and the Suharto-Nasution faction.[59] In a meeting in mid-February, Ambassador Green recommended to President Johnson that the US should 'continue to maintain a low profile', but should now accede to requests for aid 'on humanitarian grounds as well as to help prevent outbreaks of food riots and disorders'.[60]

Having resolved to assist the fledgling Suharto-Nasution regime at some point in the future, the State Department moved on to consider how best to overcome the potential political and logistical problems posed by the proposed assistance, noting that 'Any transaction on the scale of 50,000 tons [of rice], involving roughly $7 million, simply cannot be handled by [the United States Government] on a covert basis.'[61] The State Department, having decided to use Thailand as the intermediary for the provision of 'rice and other essential commodities', resolved to wait until the situation had reached a 'critical point'.[62] In the event, however, the process was expedited, and a telegram of 18th February advised that the State Department was in the 'final stages of approval' of a programme for the provision of an annual 50,000 tons of foodstuffs to help prop up the new regime.[63] A memorandum of 21st February assured President Johnson that 'few if any US initiatives to influence the course of events are apparent'.[64]

By March the position was becoming increasingly clear: Sukarno would remain, but only as a powerless figurehead. The US Deputy Chief of Mission in Jakarta, Jack Lydman, noted that recent student demonstrations had 'torn [a] hole in [the] political doctrine which identified Sukarno with [the] state'. The erstwhile symbol of national independence and unity was increasingly becoming the object of resentment and anger, and although the chances of his being toppled by 'firm army action' were 'slim', the new situation represented a 'significant improvement over [the] earlier situation'.[65] Sukarno's position was now so vulnerable that Adam Malik, a senior minister in the new regime, told Ambassador Green that an attempt by Sukarno to dismiss Suharto would actually be welcome, in so far as it would provide 'precisely the action which would incite [the] armed forces to move physically against [the] Presidium and bring about long-needed changes'.[66] On 12th March, the Embassy triumphantly reported that 'the PKI was dissolved and permanently proscribed throughout Indonesia' by an order issued on the same day by Suharto.[67] On the previous day, a reluctant Sukarno had formally handed to Suharto the authority to restore order across the country. Green's comment that 'Indonesia has just gone through its own peculiar form of military coup'[68] is particularly instructive; whilst many commentators have been content to analyse these developments in terms of an ill-defined process whereby power was transferred by some sort of consensual osmosis, the American ambassador was in little doubt that Indonesia had just undergone a military takeover. That same day, National Security Council Advisor Robert Komer proposed that the US should 'follow through and skilfully consolidate such successes', arguing that a donation of a few thousand tons of wheat or rice would have 'a psychological significance out of all proportion to the [financial] cost of the gesture', and would help to win over the new regime.[69]

During the course of March 1966, early expectations about the new regime's staunchly anti-communist orientation were confirmed, to the delight of the State Department, which observed that 'early indications are that Subandrio and other leftists will be left out [of the newly-reorganised cabinet]'.[70] Anticipating the authoritarian and military-dominated nature of the new regime, the State Department noted that 'the military ... may in the long run prove to be Indonesia's most significant "newly emerging force"'.[71] Whilst the new government would be 'concerned about [the] basic economic problems of Indonesia', it was unlikely that their concern would manifest itself in a 'reduction in [the] size of [the] civil service or army', as the new regime was likely to maintain a strong central state, and rely on 'palliative help from outside' to tackle the country's economic problems.[72] The new regime was intent on re-integrating Indonesia into the world capitalist system, and within a few months a series of reforms would transform the country into a haven for foreign investors. In a telegram of 22nd March, Rusk accepted that Indonesia might occasionally prove an 'unreliable and often unfriendly voice and vote', but maintained that the benefits of bringing Indonesia 'back into [the] real world' would far outweigh such concerns.[73]

Assessing the US Role

In much of the contemporary and subsequent literature on the extermination of the PKI in 1965-66, the US is portrayed as an interested bystander witnessing the results of an explosive internal crisis. The outcome of the crisis – the accession to power of an authoritarian dictatorship characterised by strong pro-US sympathies and a willingness to open the country to international capital – is portrayed as, in US terms, a happy if somewhat fortuitous and unintended conclusion. Scrutiny of the US role in engineering the crisis, and in cultivating relations with the army clique that would eventually seize power, reveals that the guiding hand of the CIA played an important part in manipulating Indonesian domestic politics. The long-standing hostility between the nationalists and the PKI, generally conceived in terms of an organic, purely internal contest rooted in local cultural antipathies, was actively stoked up by covert US operations. In March 1965, a National Security Council committee approved a proposal for covert actions including 'support to existing anti-Communist groups', 'black letter operations' and 'media operations', with the aim of 'portray[ing] the PKI as an increasingly ambitious, dangerous opponent of Sukarno and legitimate nationalism', to unite anti-communist elements. Some 'leading nationalist personalities' had been given 'some funds', through 'secure channels', in order to 'take obstructive action against the PKI'.[74] It was, in Peter Dale Scott's words, a 'model destabilisation plan'[75], a variant of which would be executed with similar success (though with a far lower death toll) a few years later in Chile, in the operation that would bring the dictator Augusto Pinochet to power and end parliamentary democracy in that country.

Having helped to engineer the crisis in this way, and by exacerbating Indonesia's economic problems through the withdrawal of routine economic assistance, the US went on to exert its influence to ensure that the crisis would be resolved in a manner which was favourable to American economic and strategic interests, by providing logistical and financial support to the Indonesian army to support its systematic extermination programme. In the late 1980s, the American journalist Kathy Kadane caused a minor stir when she published a series of interviews with American officials who had been serving in Indonesia during the 1960s. These included Robert Martens, a member of the US embassy's political affairs section, who admitted handing over to the Indonesian army a list of PKI members, knowing they would be tracked down and killed. In a letter to the *Washington Post*, Martens sought to play down the implications of his actions by arguing that the list – which included, in his words, 'a few thousand' names – was only a list of the party's 'leaders and senior cadre', a somewhat unconvincing explanation, given that the party's hard-core leadership was estimated to number no more than about five-hundred people at most.[76] Even right-wing commentators like Theodore Friend, whose account of the killings tends to play down the US role – astonishingly, he describes Kadane's charge of US complicity as 'presumptive' – have been unable to explain away the complicity of the US in this matter. Although Friend is unwilling to refute the plausibility of Martens' explanation (the statements 'of an honourable man must be respected'), he concludes that the consequences of supplying the information were surely not beyond the imagination of diplomatic professionals[77], and therefore apportions some blame to Martens on account of his laxity. Given the fact that the policy of deliberate mass murder was endorsed at the very highest levels of US policymaking, this interpretation is extremely generous to say the least.

Kadane dismissed any suggestion that the US might have been unaware of the scale of the slaughter, noting that the CIA was at all times monitoring the Indonesian army's communications over the state-of-the-art mobile radios it had provided to the Indonesian strategic reserve, Kostrad: 'The CIA made sure the frequencies the Army would use were known in advance to the National Security Agency [which] intercepted the broadcasts at a site in Southeast Asia, where its analysts subsequently translated them. The intercepts were then sent on to Washington'. The US, therefore, was kept fully up to date, with intercepts revealing information as specific and as detailed as 'commands from Suharto's intelligence unit to kill particular persons at given locations.'[78] This accords with the content of the declassified documentation of the *Foreign Relations of the United States of America* series which shows, as we have seen, that American officials were well aware of the nature and scale of the anti-communist campaign almost from the outset. There is not, at any stage, even one hint of concern expressed on moral grounds with regard to the systematic mass murder of at least half a million people – responses ranged from quiet, understated satisfaction to barely concealed delight. US officials provided moral support – advising the new Suharto-Nasution regime that the 'Embassy and [United States Government are] generally sympathetic with and admiring of what the Army is doing'[79] – and, just as importantly, the financial and logistical support that helped to maintain the army's Kap-Gestapu civilian front organisation, which provided the civilian-level organisational structure for the killings.

On the US Government side, the mass killing was justified in terms of Cold War policy: Deputy Undersecretary of State Ural Alexis Johns, speaking in October 1966, hailed the 'reversal of the Communist tide in the great country of Indonesia' as, along with the Vietnam war, 'the most historic turning point in Asia in this decade'[80], as Indonesia, with her considerable natural resources and vast population, would be integrated into the capitalist world on terms favourable to the United States and international financial institutions affiliated with the United States. US economic assistance would help Suharto through a potentially difficult period in 1966, helping to stabilise the regime and thus ensuring its legitimacy and longevity (see

Chapter Five, below). The savage slaughter of half a million innocent people was, it would seem, considered a price worth paying, and certainly represented good value for the economic and strategic benefits that would accrue to the United States from Suharto's violent seizure of power. President Johnson's verdict – that the accession of Suharto's New Order represented a 'magnificent story of opportunity seen and promise awakened'[81] – certainly accords with this assessment. The memoirs of the United States' most senior representatives in Jakarta treat the killings with a triumphalist sense of righteousness that neatly mirrors the stance of the US establishment. Howard Palfrey Jones, the US ambassador in Jakarta from 1958 to 1965, assessed the situation in 1965-66 in predictably ideological terms: Suharto and the Indonesian army (who were massacring tens of thousands of innocent people) represented 'the political moderates', while Sukarno (who was pleading for a cessation in the violence) represented the PKI and communist extremism.[82] Jones is full of praise for the army's assertiveness in this difficult period, contrasting this with Sukarno's increasingly desperate pleas for some sense of rational perspective to prevail ('The army acted; Sukarno ranted.').[83] Sukarno had in fact been warning the Indonesian people that he detected the secret hand of the CIA in Indonesian affairs, warning that the Agency 'are extremely clever and can use us without our being aware of it. They have years of experience, as you will discover if you read the books, *The Invisible Government*, *The CIA Story*, and Morris West's *The Ambassador*.'[84] Sukarno's protestations – dismissed by contemporary detractors as indicative of the President's anti-American paranoia, and by much of the subsequent literature as vapid 'rantings' – were in fact quite well-founded, but the President had failed to recover the initiative after the Suharto-led campaign against 'Gestapu' began in October 1965, and over these critical months effective control of the country passed into Suharto's hands. Indonesia certainly was being destabilised by foreign powers, but the destabilisation was producing an environment that was favourable to the Indonesian army – and so the army, and their affiliated newspapers, were not going to be especially exercised by it. Jones' account makes only a passing reference to the massacre, and makes no reference at all to the US efforts to destabilise Indonesia. Jones praises Suharto's new order as offering 'renewed hope' for the whole of South East Asia[85], dismissing concerns about the new regime's anti-democratic nature (elections would cost the nation 'precious time', and it was in any case obvious that 'the Suharto government would have been returned to office with a mighty mandate', so elections would have been superfluous).[86]

The memoirs of Marshall Green, the US ambassador in Jakarta at the time of the killings, take a very similar slant. In Green's account, the US is credited for having stayed out of the conflict; policymakers are praised for having incurred the risk of 'bitter recriminations against our government should the army lose out to the PKI and the Sukarnoists'.[87] Green insists that the walky-talkies supplied to the Indonesian army were 'the only material assistance we provided of a so-called covert nature', a last-resort measure because 'the lives of Nasution and Suharto were seriously threatened'.[88] This assessment does not, of course, take into account the disastrous impact of the politically-motivated decision to cut off aid to Indonesia in the months before October 1965. Nor does it take into account the National Security Council-approved decision to disseminate false propaganda (the 'media operations' described earlier in this chapter) in order to whip up anti-communist feeling in the days and weeks after the 30th September affair. Green saw the US policy of isolating and destabilising Sukarno's Indonesia as a logical and fair response to Sukarno's accommodating stance towards the PKI: 'Turning the other cheek had reached the point where it only made matters worse'.[89] That the American decision to re-open the taps of aid in support of the new regime amounted to the most essential endorsement of the Suharto junta does not seem to figure at all in Green's highly selective summary. While the killings were 'deplorable'[90], Green reminds us that the army was 'locked in a life-and-death struggle with the PKI'.[91] Green plays down the scale of the massacre, casting doubt on a very conservative estimate of a death toll of 300,000, suggesting this is 'too high' because 'many PKI members ... had fled to other parts of Java, giving rise in their native villages to assumptions that they were among the dead.'[92] Green also stresses that there was 'carnage perpetrated by both sides'[93], conveniently glossing over the enormous disparity between the relatively minor losses sustained by the

Indonesian army at the hands of the abortive 30th September rebellion and the vast numbers killed in the anti-communist purge, and implying the fallacy that the victims of the purge were combatants in a conflict with two 'sides' rather than innocent rural peasants with no connections to the 30th September group. Green also plays down the systematic nature of the killing, attributing the bloodbath primarily to 'the fact that communism ... was abhorrent to the way of life of rural Indonesia'.[94] As for the arming of Indonesian anti-communist groups, this is explained as a sensible and proportionate response to the PKI's proposal that the peasantry be provided with weapons: 'The PKI took the first step ... by lobbying for the distribution of weapons to peasants and workers'[95]; the Muslims and nationalists formed their paramilitary groups in response to the PKI's quasi-military youth, peasant and labour organisations. Rumours of communist weapons caches 'caused the Army to distribute weapons to Moslem and traditionalist groups'[96]; Green's assessment that 'the latter's firepower seemed to have greatly exceeded that of the communists'[97] is quite an understatement, and his sense of uncertainty almost certainly an affectation given that, as we have seen, he was kept fully up to date as to the nature of the anti-communist onslaught in the months after September 1965. In this regard, one aspect of Green's account is particularly galling. 'Of course,' he claims, 'We were appalled by the stories of carnage ... but they were second-or-third-hand stories we learned after the fact'.[98] Given that, as we have seen in this chapter, Green and his team were kept very well informed on the progress of the anti-PKI campaign and the precise form it was taking, this can only be dismissed as an outright lie. Ultimately, Green's dismissal of any lingering human rights concerns with regard to the anti-PKI campaign is couched in a disingenuous language of non-intervention: 'This was a highly charged emotional situation, and it would have been folly to have been drawn into the Army's life-and-death struggle with the PKI'.[99] Any slight reservations about the massacre are drowned in gushing praise for its chief perpetrator: Suharto's perceived success in managing the Indonesian economy (considered in Chapter Five) is attributed to Suharto's 'shrewd judgement, common sense, patience [and] a refinement and calmness of spirit' which Green contrasts favourably with 'Sukarno's emotionalism'[100];

later in the memoir, this assessment is simplified to a somewhat more accurate appraisal, in which Green acknowledges the significance of Suharto's 'commanding position'[101] (i.e. dictatorship) in enabling him to force through highly unpopular structural adjustment policies as the pre-condition for bail-out loans from the International Monetary Fund, which would bring at least some semblance of stability to the Indonesian economy. Acknowledging the strength of US influence in the new Indonesia under Suharto, Green recalls that 'we were at pains to keep down the size and conspicuousness of our presence', as this was the 'sensible thing to do politically and psychologically'.[102] In summary, Green states, 'we rather lucked out in Indonesia ... It was indeed all rather miraculous.'[103]

From a tactical perspective, the techniques adopted by the US in Indonesia constitute a marked shift in the United States' strategic approach to protecting and enhancing its global hegemony in the post-War era. If the CIA's support for the unsuccessful PRRI uprising in 1958 belonged to the same genre of clumsy power politics as the Agency's misguided sponsorship of the abortive Bay of Pigs invasion of Cuba in 1961, the cultivation of links with the Indonesian military throughout the 1960s may be seen as part of a distinct and more sophisticated approach which would come to characterise US foreign policy in the Cold War era and beyond. Rather than forging links with dubious, marginal rebel groups out of touch with the centres of power, the US would cultivate relationships of mutual convenience with military establishments at the heart of effective power, as well as establishing strong links with domestic media outlets in order to influence public opinion. This would become particularly pertinent in view of the long-term effect on US political culture of the Vietnam War (1959-1975), which provoked a peace movement of such significant scale and impact that much of the American establishment came to view direct military intervention by US soldiers as a politically dangerous means of pursuing Cold War objectives. With direct intervention unpopular, and the engagement of proxy armies discredited by PRRI and the Bay of Pigs, the only credible, proven strategy that remained was a return to the technique successfully employed in the overthrow of Iran's reformist premier Mohammad Mossadeq in 1953. On that occasion, a CIA-engineered coup overthrew a popular civilian politician and replaced him with a senior army General who shut down the country's democratic institutions and effected a reorientation of Iran's economic policy in a direction favourable to US and European oil interests, and to US global geopolitical Cold War priorities. In Iran's case, the necessary backdrop of domestic instability had been brought about by a combination of internal political conflict and the machinations of the declining regional imperial powerhouse, the British; over the course of the 1960s and the 1970s, successive US administrations would make it their business to engineer such crises, developing a standard *modus operandi* for removing troublesome regimes. Allowing for some simplification, the strategy may be broadly summarised as follows: a combination of economic pressure and media manipulation would be used to destabilise the country and exacerbate existing social and political tensions, while the local military was furnished with extravagant aid packages; once the domestic instability had reached crisis point, a military takeover would be effected in order to 'rescue' the country, usually involving the installation of a military 'strongman' as head of state (there would then follow a realignment of domestic economic policy in accordance with US priorities accompanied, to a greater or lesser extent, by severe political repression and human rights abuse). The United States did not have a conspiratorial hand in the 'Gestapu' affair, and it provided relatively little extra support for the Indonesian army during the massacres. However, the US made a telling contribution to Suharto's rise to power by cultivating strong links with the Suharto-Nasution group over a number of years, and forging a community of interests based on a shared ideological outlook. Through years of assistance to the Indonesian military and its affiliated civilian front groups (most notably Kap-Gestapu), along with the economic and political de-stabilisation of Indonesia (through aid cuts and 'media operations', respectively) the United States managed to shape developments in such a way as to bring about an outcome that was favourable to her global economic and strategic priorities. In this sense, the Indonesian policy may be seen as marking a new, more mature stage in US imperialism, after the bungled efforts of PRRI and the Bay of Pigs, and a forerunner to similar operations that would install murderous military dictatorships in Chile,

Argentina and Brazil, and across much of Central America, in the 1970s and 1980s.

Notes
1 Foreign Relations of the United States, 1952-54, Volume XII, Document 1066, cited in Kolko, *Confronting the Third World*, p174.
2 Roosa, *Pretext for Mass Murder*, p179.
3 National Security Council 'Special Report on Indonesia, January 1959' ('US Policy on Indonesia', NSC 5901, 16th January, 1959), cited in Roosa, *Pretext for Mass Murder*, pp181-182.
4 Roosa, *Pretext for Mass Murder*, p183.
5 Roosa, *Pretext for Mass Murder*, p182.
6 Roosa, *Pretext for Mass Murder*, p183.
7 Joint message from State Department, Agency for International Development, US Information Agency, Defense Deparment, 12th July 1962, cited in Roosa, *Pretext for Mass Murder*, p183.
8 State Department Policy Planning Council, 'Role of the Military in Underdeveloped Areas', 25th January 1963, cited in Roosa, *Pretext for Mass Murder*, p185.
9 Howard Palfrey Jones, *Indonesia: The Possible Dream* (Singapore: AYU MAS PTE, 1977), p299.
10 Scott, 'The United States and the Overthrow of Sukarno, 1965-67', p253.
11 Jones, *The Possible Dream*, p324, cited in Scott, 'The United States and the Overthrow of Sukarno, 1965-67', p253.
12 US State Department *Military Assistance Facts* 1st May 1966, cited in Scott, 'The United States and the Overthrow of Sukarno, 1965-67', p255.
13 Scott, 'The United States and the Overthrow of Sukarno, 1965-67', pp257-258.
14 Friend, *Indonesian Destinies*, p102, citing personal account of George Benson.
15 Memorandum for President Johnson, 1st October 1965, Foreign Relations of the United States 1964-1968, Volume XXVI, Indonesia; Malaysia-Singapore; Philippines, documents 142-164 (hereafter 'FRUS'), Document 142
16 Ibid.
17 Telephone conversation (Ball/McNamara) 1st October 1965, FRUS Doc 143.
18 Telephone conversation (Ball/Fulbright) 1st October 1965, FRUS Doc 144.
19 'American-Indonesian Relations' presentation by Howard P. Jones at Chiefs of Mission Conference, Baguio, Philippines, Howard P. Jones Papers, box 21, Hoover Institution Archives, 12, cited in Roosa, *Pretext for Mass Murder*, p190.
20 Telephone conversation (Ball/Rusk) 2nd October 1965, FRUS Doc 145.

21 Telegram (Jakarta to Washington) 5th October 1965, FRUS Doc 147.
22 Ibid.
23 Telegram (Washington to Jakarta) 6th October 1965, FRUS Doc 148.
24 Ibid.
25 Telegram (Washington to Jakarta) 13th October 1964, FRUS Doc 153.
26 Ibid.
27 Telegram (Jakarta to Washington) 15th October 1965, FRUS Doc 155.
28 Ibid.
29 Telegram (Jakarta to Washington) 17th October 1965, FRUS Doc 156.
30 Telegram (Jakarta to Washington) 20th October 1965, FRUS Doc 158.
31 Ibid.
32 Telegram (Washington to Jakarta) 22nd October 1965, FRUS Doc 159.
33 See Chapter One. Especially thorough analyses of the various conflicting explanations for the 30th September events appear in Roosa, *Pretext for Mass Murder*, Chapter 2 and Crouch, *Army and Politics*, Chapter 4.
34 Telegram (Washington to Jakarta) 22nd October 1965, FRUS Doc 159.
35 State Department internal memorandum (Bundy to President Johnson) 22nd October 1965, FRUS Doc 160.
36 Telegram (Washington to Jakarta) 29th October 1965, FRUS Doc 163.
37 State Department internal memorandum (Nuechterlein/Friedman) 30th October 1965, FRUS Doc 164.
38 Telegram (Jakarta to Washington) 1st November 1965, FRUS Doc 165.
39 State Department internal memorandum (Cuthell/Bundy) 3rd November 1965, FRUS Doc 167.
40 Ibid.
41 Telegram (Jakarta to Washington) 4th November 1965, FRUS Doc 169.
42 Telegram (Bangkok to Washington) 5th November 1965, FRUS Doc 171.
43 State Department internal memorandum (prepared by the CIA) 5th November 1965, FRUS Doc 172.
44 Ibid.
45 Ibid.
46 Ibid.
47 Telegram (Bangkok to Washington) 11th November 1965, FRUS Doc 173.
48 Telegram (Medan to Washington) 16th November 1965, FRUS Doc 174.
49 State Department internal memorandum (prepared for the National Security Council 303 Committee)17th November 1965, FRUS Doc 175.
50 Ibid.
51 Intelligence memorandum (prepared by the Office of Current Intelligence) 22nd November 1965, FRUS Doc 178.
52 Telegram (Jakarta to Washington) 2nd December 1965, FRUS Doc 179.
53 State Department internal memorandum (Blouin/Friedman) 13th December 1965, FRUS Doc 183.
54 Telegram (Washington to Jakarta) 16th December 1965, FRUS Doc 184.
55 Telegram (Jakarta to Washington) 22nd December 1965, FRUS Doc 186.

56 State Department internal memorandum (Joint Chiefs of Staff to McNamara) 30th December 1965, FRUS Doc 187.
57 Telegram (Washington to Jakarta) 20th January 1966, FRUS Doc 189.
58 Memorandum of conversation (Rusk/Green/Goodspeed) 14th February 1966, FRUS Doc 191.
59 Briefing notes for President Johnson 15th February 1966, FRUS Doc 193.
60 Memorandum of conversation (President Johnson/Bundy/Green/Komer) 15th February 1966, FRUS Doc 194.
61 Telegram (Washington to Bangkok) 15th Februray 1966, FRUS Doc 195
62 Ibid.
63 Telegram (Washington to Wellington) 18th February 1966, FRUS Doc 196.
64 State Department internal memorandum (Bundy and Cooper to President Johnson) 21st February 1966, FRUS Doc 197.
65 Telegram (Jakarta to Washington) 4th March 1966, FRUS Doc 198.
66 Telegram (Jakarta to Washington) 10th March 1966, FRUS Doc 199.
67 Telegram (Jakarta to Washington) 12th March 1966, FRUS Doc 200.
68 Ibid.
69 State department internal memorandum (Komer to President Johnson) 12th March 1966, FRUS Doc 201.
70 State department internal memorandum (Berger to Rusk) 14th March 1966, FRUS Doc 202.
71 Ibid. This is a gloating reference to Sukarno's use of the term 'Newly-Emerging Forces' to describe the bloc of emerging Asian developing countries. This group would be characterised by staunch anti-imperialism and a non-anligned policy with respect to the Cold War. Sukarno had envisaged that Indonesia would take a leaderhip position in this bloc.
72 Telegram (Washington to Jakarta) 17th March 1966, FRUS Doc 203.
73 Telegram (Washington to Jakarta) 22nd March 1966, FRUS Doc 204.
74 State Department internal memorandum, 'Memorandum Prepared for the 303 Committee' 23rd February 1965, in Foreign Relations of the United States 1964-1968 Doc. 26, 234-237, cited in Roosa, *Pretext for Mass Murder*, p191.
75 Scott, 'The United States and the Overthrow of Sukarno, 1965-67', p259.
76 Roosa, *Pretext for Mass Murder*, p195, citing Robert Martens, Letter to the Editor, *Washington Post*, 2nd June 1990.
77 Friend, *Indonesian Destinies*, p118.
78 Kathy Kadane, Letter to the Editor, *New York Review of Books*, 10th April 1997, cited in Roosa, *Pretext for Mass Murder*, p195
79 Telegram (Jakarta to Washington) 4th November 1965, FRUS Doc 169.
80 *US Department of State Bulletin*, 24th October 1966, 640, cited in Kolko, *Confronting the Third World*, p181.
81 Letter from President Lyndon Jonson to James A Linen, December 1967, LBJ Library, cited in Pilger, *New Rulers of the World*, p42.
82 Jones, *The Possible Dream*, p390.

83 Jones, *The Possible Dream*, p390.
84 Cited in Jones, *The Possible Dream*, p392.
85 Jones, *The Possible Dream*, p416.
86 Ibid, pp409-410.
87 Marshall Green, *Indonesia: Crisis and Transformation 1965-68* (Washington: Compass Press, 1990), p64.
88 Ibid, p69.
89 Ibid, p13.
90 Ibid, p58.
91 Ibid, pp70-71.
92 Ibid, p61.
93 Ibid, p155.
94 Ibid, p59.
95 Ibid, pp58-59.
96 Ibid, pp58-59.
97 Ibid, p59.
98 Ibid, p155.
99 Ibid, p155.
100 Ibid, p104.
101 Ibid, p114.
102 Ibid, p119.
103 Ibid, pp155-156.

CHAPTER FOUR

'Confrontation' and 'Psychological Warfare'
Britain and Indonesia in 1965-66

In September 1963, the new federation of Malaysia – comprising former British colonial possessions in the Malay peninsula and Borneo, as well as former Dutch conquests in the North – declared its independence. Federation was intended to permit Britain to decolonise in South East Asia while retaining a significant power base to protect her considerable economic interests in the region. The military base at Singapore, and the political and legal institutions of the new Malaysian federation, would provide the British with effective, and relatively cost-efficient, means of preserving their influence in South East Asia in the post-colonial era. Several months earlier, in January 1963, the Indonesian Foreign Minister Subandrio had warned that the Indonesian response to the formation of a Malaysian state would be one of *Konfrontasi* – 'confrontation'. While the Sukarno government's hostility to Malaysia was attributable in part to crude chauvinistic nationalism – a belief that the Borneo territories should rightfully form part of neighbouring Indonesian Kalimantan (with the exception of the North Borneo territories, which should remain independent), and a cynical desire to re-assert the liberation-era rhetoric of fervent anti-colonialism may both have played a part – the basis of the Indonesian policy was rooted in sound, sober thinking and well-founded fears about the potential threat posed to Indonesia's security and her position in the region. The Revolutionary Government of the Indonesian Republic (PRRI) rebellion of 1958, which had shaken the Jakarta government with its threat of regional secession, had received considerable support from Malayan and Singaporean quarters, and Sukarno had expressed grave concerns about the likely political orientation of the new state, which he believed would amount to a British neo-colonial stronghold in the region. The Malaysian federation would preserve, on Indonesia's doorstep, the corrupt monarchical order that the

Indonesians themselves had struggled so long to overthrow. This was a view shared by many of Sukarno's supporters among the country's influential nationalist element, who were affronted that the formation of the new federation had been pushed through without even consulting Indonesia. The significant backing provided for the 1958 PRRI rebellion by powerful figures in Singapore and Malaya only underlined Sukarno's view that the new federation would be a troublesome, destabilising influence, posing a substantial threat to the security and prosperity of the Indonesian nation. In an autobiography first published in 1965, Sukarno outlined the reasoning behind his hostility to the new federation:

'We didn't fear the amalgamation of 10 million people, but it became obvious Malaysia was not to be a friendly neighbour. One article in the treaty of formation states the new country "will afford to the United Kingdom the right to continue to maintain military bases and permit that government to make use of those bases as it may consider necessary ... for the preservation of peace in Southeast Asia".

Fresh in our minds are those demonstrations of foreign pilots who operated from bases surrounding us – bases like that in Singapore; British territory; territory governed by Tunku Abdul Rahman, an avowed anti-Indonesian who protected, subsidised, and still shelters in Kuala Lumpur many rebels who revolted against me in 1958. Is that not ground for us to be on our guard, particularly when these colonies which ring us have been hastily and hostilely cemented together by steamroller tactics? Particularly when British military installations on that soil make it clear Malaysia isn't truly a sovereign, fully independent Asian nation but, in reality, the result of the brain of the British? Their 'gift' of independence was wrapped in a form of new colonialism. Colonialism wasn't retreating in my backyard, just changing shape.'[1]

The Malaysian declaration was greeted with violence in Jakarta – the British embassy and over two-hundred staff houses in Jakarta were burned down. Malaysia broke off diplomatic relations with Indonesia in protest at the violence; in turn, Indonesia severed all relations with Malaya and Singapore. As these regions handled nearly half the nation's exports, this was a move which served to exacerbate Indonesia's acute economic problems. Sukarno sought to initiate a nationwide mobilisation that would provide a political solution to his mounting domestic problems, uniting the military and the PKI; the former would benefit from increased budgets, and the latter would see its reputation enhanced by the adoption, at state level, of an anti-imperialist line supported by both China and the Soviet Union. The accompanying rhetoric would be suitably belligerent – on 25th September 1963, Sukarno declared bullishly that Indonesia would 'gobble Malaysia raw' (*ganjang Malaysia*).

Over the ensuing months, Indonesian troops carried out a series of small, strategic raids in the border regions of the new state, ostensibly in support of indigenous nationalist elements within the new state that were hostile to the new Malaysian federation. British and Commonwealth troops were sent in to protect the newly-independent Malaysian state from Indonesian incursions. This small-scale but potentially explosive conflict came to be known by Subandrio's term – the 'Confrontation'. Once the Suharto clique had completed the greater part of their campaign of extermination against the PKI by April 1966, they took steps to wind down and eventually end the conflict. The Generals were not taken in by the policy of Confrontation, which they viewed as a legacy of the Sukarno period and a product of the anti-Western nationalism of a bygone era; the Suharto group recognised that Indonesia, crippled by economic and political turmoil, was in no position to pursue a potentially unwinnable campaign against the combined might of Britain and her Commonwealth allies, however justified her concerns about the threat posed by the new Malaysian federation. In any case, the political orientation of the new regime was unequivocally pro-Western – even if some of the anti-imperialist rhetoric was retained for propaganda purposes (especially where anti-Chinese incitement was called for) – and the defence of indigenous rebels in Borneo and Malaya had no place in the vision of Suharto's 'New Order'.

Britain's relations with Indonesia during the massacres must, therefore, be considered in the context of the Confrontation of 1963-1966. The Confrontation presented a peculiar problem for the British government with respect to their stance on the developments arising after the 30th September 1965 affair. On the one hand, Britain was at war with the Indonesian army over Malaysia; on the other hand, Britain's strategic ambitions for the region, in Cold War terms, matched those of the United States – the British desired the destruction of the PKI by the army, and wished to support the army's ascendancy accordingly. The issue was complicated further by the fact that senior elements within the Indonesian army were themselves opposed to their involvement in Malaysia. As we shall see, therefore, the secret diplomacy of the period was characterised by a series of tentative approaches on both sides. As the killings in Indonesia continued and the strength and political orientation of the new regime became apparent, so the British stance gradually softened commensurately, until eventually a solid relationship of mutual support had crystallised, paving the way for decades of British support for the Suharto dictatorship. Interestingly, however, the British government did not consider the military engagement in Malaysia sufficient to preclude active covert support for the anti-communist campaign in the wake of the 'Gestapu' mutiny. A liaison office of the Indonesian army in Bangkok informed the British that they need not take the Confrontation too seriously – although the Indonesian army was carrying out its orders, it had no intention of staging a major war. So, while the British were concerned to protect their interests in Malaysia, they endorsed and prioritised, from the very outset, the perceived strategic need to have the PKI destroyed in Indonesia. Britain's most significant contribution to the mass killings came in the form of the so-called 'psywar' – psychological warfare – operations before and after the 30th September mutiny, whereby false news stories about PKI atrocities, past and future, were circulated by British agencies in order to stir up anti-communist anger among nationalist and Muslim youths.

The Foreign Office and the '30th September Movement'

Like their American counterparts, British foreign policy officials were anticipating a Nasution-led anti-communist coup in the summer of 1965. The British ambassador to Thailand, Anthony Rumbold, advised the Foreign Office on 16th June of a meeting with the Malaysian ambassador Ibrahim Ya'acob, who 'seems to be quite well informed about the alleged plot against Sukarno', which involved 'a *coup d'état* ... by or on behalf of Nasution and other anti-communists'.[2] In Indonesia itself, the British Ambassador Andrew Gilchrist noted a 'creeping barrage of sabre-rattling' in Jakarta.[3] When the mutiny of 30th September happened, the embassy was in no doubt that it was intended as a pre-emptive move against a Nasution coup – the PKI had a 'desperate and drastic survival plan to anticipate an inevitable army takeover by force'.[4] Rumours of Sukarno's serious illness may have prompted Untung and his associates into action, but the nature and extent of the PKI's involvement was ultimately 'of no consequence': the Indonesian army 'could not have hoped for a more perfect, if expensive, excuse to wipe out the PKI'. The communists were poorly armed, so the army 'should find little difficulty in crushing the PKI fairly quickly'. This assessment, produced less than a week after the 'coup' in Jakarta, shows the Foreign Office to be completely in tune with the thinking of the Indonesian army, understanding that there was no likelihood that the 30th September events would simply be treated as an internal army matter – the mutiny would be used as a pretext for the destruction of the entire party and its elimination as a viable actor in Indonesian domestic politics.

The developments of October 1965 required a flexible approach, so the British decided that, strictly as a matter of 'short-term policy', the requirements of the Confrontation would be subjugated, for the foreseeable future, to the overriding need to ensure a positive outcome in Indonesia. A memorandum from the Commonwealth Relations Office emphasised that Britain 'did not want to distract the Indonesian army by getting them engaged in fighting in Borneo'. In the meantime, the principal aim of British policy in Indonesia would be to 'spread alarm and despondency ... and aggravate and prolong the present crisis' in order to 'encourage anti-Communist Indonesians to more vigorous action in the hopes of crushing Communism in Indonesia altogether'. British media organisations in Indonesia would do their utmost to 'discredit the PKI in the eyes of the Indonesian people'. The memorandum suggests that an effective way of doing this would be to emphasise 'PKI cruelty in murdering [the] Generals and [their] families', while pandering to nationalist sentiment by presenting the 30th September affair as an example of 'Chinese interference' in Indonesian affairs; the propaganda campaign should portray the senior Generals as patriotic heroes and emphasise that the communists were 'subverting Indonesia as agents of foreign communists'.[5] British policy was unequivocally committed to the establishment of a military regime in Indonesia, on the basis that the only perceived alternative was a communist government in Jakarta. An Embassy memorandum on 13th October stressed that a communist government would 'inevitably be worse' than a military dictatorship: 'We see every advantage in letting the Generals get on with clobbering the Communists'. The memorandum also suggests to the Foreign Office that the 'British papers should make the points summarised above' and, presumably, not concern themselves with the human rights implications of Britain's position.[6]

By mid-October, British officials had pieced together a relatively coherent explanation of recent events informed to some significant extent by the Indonesian army's own, self-serving perspective. The Joint Malaysia/Indonesia Department was briefed about 'growing evidence that the Indonesian Army leaders believe that the Indonesian Communist Party (PKI) was deeply implicated in the coup of 30th September, and that China also had a hand in this'.[7] At this stage, however, the Foreign Office was quite adamant that the fervently nationalistic ideological framework of the Nasution clique precluded any early settlement with regard to Malaysia; despite the Generals' pro-Western inclinations, it would be 'over-optimistic to believe that [the Nasution clique] might be willing to call off confrontation'.[8] The Foreign Office understood that 'any obvious sympathy for the West ... would weaken them politically', an unnecessary risk at this sensitive time.[9] Towards the end of October, a memorandum from Washington suggested that the British should give the Generals assurances that, should they find themselves needing to withdraw troops from Borneo to reinforce the domestic anti-communist extermination campaign, their positions in Borneo would not be at risk of an attack from Britain.[10]

By November, British officials were meeting with members of the new regime and were being kept fully informed of the nature and scale of the anti-communist campaign. A conversation with General Achmad Junus Mokoginta on 9th November informed the Foreign Office that an estimated three hundred thousand PKI members were being pursued in Sumatra, amid concerns that their indefinite detention would pose a 'security problem'. Mokoginta advised that, since early October, the 'Army has been rounding up and imprisoning both leaders and rank and file at the rate of about 3,000 a week'. A 'return of law and order to the area' was expected by about Christmas time. Army 'indoctrination teams' were at work, whipping up anti-communist sentiment in order to maintain a high level of civilian involvement in the campaign. The techniques of these 'indoctrination teams' included the playing of recordings of alleged confessions by PKI members implicated in the 'Gestapu' affair to mass audiences in public places. According to Mokoginta, these techniques had proved so effective that some PKI rank and file offered to track down and denounce their own leaders. The General insisted that the present momentum would have to be maintained, as any resurgence of the PKI would lead to 'tremendous frictions' within Indonesia. The British report concluded that it was 'impossible to resist the conclusion that, so far as [Mokoginta] was concerned, once bitten, twice shy'.[11] It was at this point that British representatives provided express assurances that hostilities over Malaysia would be suspended in order to assist the Indonesian army by allowing them to pursue their anti-communist campaign with the maximum possible efficiency: 'The army could ... be assured that while they were engaged in their present task, we did not, on our side, propose to step up confrontation, nor to undertake offensive operations against them'.[12] Mokoginta in turn indicated a willingness to end Confrontation, but it was agreed that secrecy would be best for the time being, in view of the risk that the thawing of relations with Britain might create political problems for the Generals domestically.

With the tension of Confrontation now eased, British officials met with the Indonesian General Sukendro in a secret meeting also attended by the Malaysian foreign minister, Dato Ghazali. On behalf of the Indonesian army, Sukendro requested outside help in order to 'consolidate its position' domestically, and emphasised the systematic and organised nature of the army's domestic campaign. The minutes report that 'a comprehensive plan of action covering all aspects of the Army's strategy against the Communists has already been prepared and distributed to Army Commanders for action' and 'considerations are being made to meet the clamour of the nationalists and the religious elements for arms'; 'steps have already been taken to supply arms to [various Muslim organisations including Ansor]'.[13] The minutes are suitably euphemistic with regard to the treatment being meted out to the communists, who were being 'dislodged' and 'kept under control' by the army. The Ministry of Defence, meanwhile, was advancing the case for enhancing 'the psychological warfare aspect of the present to-do in Indonesia', commenting positively on an earlier Commonwealth Relations Office telegram which 'did not exclude immediate action in respect of unattributable propaganda or psychological warfare activities', and suggesting a possible role in this regard for a 'Deception Action Group'.[14]

Despite British assurances, the Generals remained apprehensive about re-directing military resources from the Malaysian stand-off to the domestic anti-communist campaign. In November, Mokoginta's Deputy Chief of Staff Soesatjo advised that only 50% of available forces were being deployed in the anti-PKI campaign, with the other half being held in reserve against possible British action over Malaysia. The US military attaché had expressed doubts about the accuracy of Soesatjo's claim of a 50-50 split in resource allocation, but for his part Andrew Gilchrist was convinced of the 'sincerity of [the] Indonesian suspicions', and advised the Foreign Office that Britain should 'try to allay them where possible'.[15] The Embassy had previously expressed concern that the tentative, unofficial truce would be sabotaged by the pro-Sukarno minister Dr Subandrio, whom Gilchrist believed to be attempting to 'tie up the Army to the maximum extent against the British so that their effort against the PKI will be correspondingly weakened'.[16] Despite a growing willingness to win the trust and confidence of the Generals, a Foreign Office brief of 16th November emphasised that any aid offered to the Generals should not be unconditional, warning that 'premature aid to the Generals should not give them the impression that they can continue confrontation and at the same time win the international support and help that Sukarno has lost'.[17] Such considerations were secondary, however, to the overriding objective of supporting the army in its anti-communist campaign of extermination. In a telegram to the Embassy in Washington, the Foreign Office expressed concern that the 'Generals seem to be losing momentum', and suggested that the United States and Great Britain should come to an agreement, sooner rather than later, with regard to 'a common policy on material aid whether in minor ways ... or in rice supplies'.[18] At an Area Meeting in Kuala Lumpur on 26th November, opinion was divided as to the true strength of the PKI. While some officials believed that the developments of recent weeks had exposed the PKI as a 'paper tiger', others were convinced of the existence of a 'second or third layer of leadership which ... could still cause a lot of trouble at a suitable opportunity in the future', especially given the ongoing economic problems in Indonesia. The time was now right for the direct involvement of the British in serious talks with the Generals, without the need for a third party such as Australia to act as a go-between.[19]

Edward Peck, head of the Southeast Asia Division of the Foreign Office, advised his Foreign Office colleagues that the Indonesian 'situation has developed on encouraging lines', so much so, in fact, that Peck was worried that the US will have been so impressed with the Generals' anti-communist campaign as to forgo any insistence on a return with respect to Confrontation. Peck even suggested warning Britain's American allies that a failure to achieve a negotiated 'withering away of confrontation along peaceful lines' might force Britain to consider a 'sharper counter-action, including graduated military action'.[20] Mindful of Britain's junior position within the US-Great Britain relationship, and conscious of the primacy of the anti-communist struggle over Britain's concerns about Confrontation, Peck's Foreign Office colleagues did not take up his suggestion. Developments within Indonesia were, after all, going extremely well. On 30th November, the Embassy reported to the Foreign Office that the Indonesian army was 'primarily concerned with the elimination of the PKI and with putting this house in order' – the army was not taking any steps to address the country's economic problems directly, although it was likely that the Generals believed that the removal of trade unions would help to solve the country's economic problems.[21] At a meeting of officials from Australia, New Zealand and the United States, the US ambassador Berger recalled how in an earlier meeting 'he had said that only a miracle could save Indonesia from the PKI. That miracle had happened.' The mass murder campaign had far exceeded American expectations: 'US thinking had been that the Army would stand aside from any fighting, leaving the PKI to struggle with the Moslems. In fact, it now seemed that an anti-Communist revolution was now in progress, irreversibly'.[22] By this point it had become abundantly clear that the continued ascendancy of the army would lead to a military regime, and the end of any hope of democratic or representative government in Indonesia. The Australian High Commissioner to Malaysia, Allan Eastman, accurately summed up the shared position of the participants when he observed that 'any regime would unquestionably serve Western interests better than a PKI regime'. As the parties discussed the pro-Western orientation of the incipient new regime, the American Deputy Director of the Office of Southwest Pacific Affairs, Francis Underhill, set out three elements of the relationship between the US and the new Suharto-led regime: the 'Pentagon link' (the 'community of feeling between American and Indonesian military officers; many of the latter had been trained in the United States ...'), the 'State Department link' (considered 'incomplete' as the Indonesian army had thus far held back from overt political discussions with the State Department) and a third element which remains classified. Edward Peck suggested offering 'economic carrots' to the new regime, adding that 'we should threaten a stick' if these were to fail. The British proposed approaching the Generals with a proposal entailing a reduction in offensive deployment in Malaysia in return for a reduction of Commonwealth troops on the Kalimantan border – a 'tacit disengagement, leading to a permanent settlement'.[23] However, a Foreign Office memorandum of 4th December 1965 acknowledged the secondary status of ending the Confrontation; the US in particular had insisted that the Generals were 'pre-occupied with domestic problems', and Confrontation was very much a 'minor subsidiary issue' compared with the requirement of providing unflinching support for the anti-communist campaign.[24] As December wore on, though, the Embassy advocated an increase of 'non-official contacts' with the new Suharto regime, in order to 'help create an atmosphere of goodwill'.[25]

1966: Relations Crystallise

When the Foreign Office learned of the US plans to supply the Generals with short-range radio equipment, initial consternation was met by reassurances from the Embassy in Washington: 'it will *not* come to public knowledge'. The transaction would be 'completely clandestine', with the US State Department promising that it would merely provide a 'no comment' response if questioned about it.[26] Logistical support was identified by the Foreign Office and the State Department as an important means of obtaining the confidence of the new regime. In this regard, the Foreign Office revised an August 1965 decision to refuse a request by the Indonesian army for Rolls Royce engines and other British equipment for use on Fokker Friendship aircraft. A Foreign Office brief of 7th January 1966 advised ministers to 'reconsider the August decision [to block the sales]' in view of 'the changed situation in Indonesia after the attempted rebellion of 30 September' and the 'possibility that the Indonesians may be starting to make overtures for better bilateral relations with Britain and that a concession on the Friendships would foster this'.[27] The Foreign Office was probably persuaded by the fear, expressed in a memorandum sent on the previous day from the British Embassy at The Hague, warning that there would be 'quite an outcry' if the 'Indonesians turn elsewhere for aircraft, and specifically the Russians ... [due to] unnecessary intransigence on our part'.[28] The decision to block the equipment sales was finally reversed on 8th February, with the Foreign Secretary seeking to play down the significance of the gesture – while the aircraft could admittedly be easily converted for military use, the new acquisitions would not 'represent a serious addition to Indonesia's military strength'.[29] On the broader question of economic assistance, however, the British were, in mid-January, prepared to bide their time. Any decision would have to be delayed pending the outcome of the power struggle between Sukarno and the increasingly emboldened military clique: 'we are in a position to deal with whatever regime emerges, whether it be the military or the civilian faction ... or some combination of both'.[30] In early February, Britain's policy on Indonesia, with respect to the political aspect of the 'internal struggle', was 'primarily one of wait and see'.[31] Later that month, the Commonwealth Relations Office warned: 'It is clear that Sukarno is ... seeking to restore the status quo ante of 30 September'.[32] However, they need not have worried. In the months after the 'coup', Indonesia's ailing President made a number of speeches seeking to defend his vision of the Indonesian Revolution, and urging a proportionate response against the 30th September plotters and their accomplices. In the face of the army-sanctioned anti-communist hysteria, Sukarno made a desperate plea for common sense to prevail. With reference to the outrageous press stories about PKI cruelty on 30th September, the embattled President asked: 'Does the journalist think we're stupid? What's his point? To stir up hatred! Does it make sense, I mean, does it make sense that a penis was sliced one hundred times by razors? ... Is our nation of such low quality that the newspapers write about imaginary things?'[33] His protestations were drowned out by the combined fury of the Muslim youth groups and the army-run newspapers, who viewed all-out violent retribution as the only acceptable solution to the treachery of 'Gestapu'. Newspaper stories included false allegations about a planned purge of anti-communists, in which electric chairs would be used against victims. An exasperated Sukarno pleaded: 'Now, then, look at this! Over and over it's the same thing. Yes, you know what I'm referring to. It's always Gestapu, Gestapu, Gestapu, Gestapu, Gestapu, razors, razors, razors, razors, razors, a grave for a thousand people, a grave for a thousand people, a grave for a thousand people, electric chair, electric chair, electric chair – over and over again, the same thing!'[34] Sukarno's pleas fell on deaf ears, and his political marginalisation in the months after 30th September was a logical consequence of the shift in effective power during this period. It was the Suharto-Nasution clique that now controlled the press as well as the guns, and once the PKI was eliminated it was only logical that the former should take formal political control of the country.

In March 1966, a Foreign Office brief to a congressional parliamentary conference in Bermuda provided a succinct appraisal of the British view of the power struggle which had been played out over the preceding five months. The 'Indonesian Communists, who began [the power struggle], and now have suffered most, are unlikely for many years to regain their former ascendancy'. Although this 'needless suffering' was 'deeply regrettable', it had at least served to 'reduce the already dwindling Indonesian pressure on British and Commonwealth troops defending Malaysia'.[35] Although Suharto's position was looking increasingly assured, the Embassy was still urging caution; on 22nd March, Gilchrist advised the Foreign Office that a reference, in a BBC newsreel, to Suharto's foreign minister Adam Malik 'being compelled to seek foreign aid from the West' should be dropped for fear of potential repercussions with respect to Suharto's nationalist credentials in Indonesia; this sort of wording should be 'dropped for good'.[36] Within a couple of months, the British would join the Americans in providing economic support to prop up a regime which had just organised the systematic murder of about half a million of its own people; a Foreign Office telegram in May 1966 advised that the British government 'have offered the Indonesians £1million aid, which they have accepted, and have reasonable grounds for hoping that important dividends will accrue to us in the Confrontation field.'.[37]

Assessing the British Role

It's position as the erstwhile colonial powerhouse of South East Asia meant Britain had a stake in Indonesian developments out of all proportion to its power to influence events decisively. The Indonesian situation was, accordingly, monitored with keen interest. Nevertheless, some British officials claim to have been taken by surprise by the events of September and October 1965. A memorandum from Herbert Stanley to the Foreign Office on 19th November 1965 records Stanley's apparent bewilderment at the PKI's involvement in the 30th September mutiny: 'Why the PKI could not wait to collect their inheritance, but let themselves in for the 30th September coup, is one of the great mysteries of the whole affair'.[38] Stanley's bemusement is somewhat surprising; Gilchrist's comments in June 1965 (with regard to the 'creeping barrage of sabre-rattling') indicate that the Embassy was well aware of the menace of the threatened Generals' coup that was anticipated in many quarters in September and October 1965, and the Embassy's uncertainty as to the extent of the PKI's role in the 30th September affair is also well-documented in the Foreign Office correspondence. It is unlikely that British officials were particularly surprised by the developments in Indonesia which began with the 30th September mutiny. As early as November 1964, a draft briefing ahead of a conference with US officials showed that the Foreign Office believed 'there might be much to be said for encouraging a premature PKI coup during Sukarno's lifetime ... [leading to] the collapse of the PKI'.[39] The Foreign Office was certainly, from the very outset, in tune with US strategic thinking with regard to the economic importance of the region: a Foreign Office memorandum of 1964 noted that the Malaysia/Indonesia region produced nearly 85% of the world's natural rubber, over 45%

of the world's tin, 65% of its copper and 23% of its chromium ore.[40] Despite Britain's declining power on the world stage, this was one area in which the British position, converging fully with that of the United States, could find expression in the form of a deliberate policy of propaganda and logistical support aimed at achieving Cold War objectives shared by both parties in the so-called 'special relationship'.

The eventual settlement of the Confrontation issue – it was resolved peacefully in August 1966 – is beyond the immediate scope of this study. A recent book by David Easter, *Britain and the Confrontation with Indonesia*, provides a thorough and detailed analysis of this most peculiar of conflicts. Easter is quite unequivocal in his conclusions with regard to the British position on the massacre: Great Britain did 'all it could to encourage the destruction of the PKI'.[41] In November 1965, a Foreign Office brief confirmed that Britain had been feeding false news stories, linking the PKI and China with the 30th September mutiny, into ordinary news outlets in Indonesia.[42] A 'Political Warfare Co-Coordinator', Norman Reddaway, fed news stories to contacts in Singapore, Kuala Lumpur and Hong Kong. The stories would be put out to the world's media, and work their way back to Indonesia through ordinary news sources. In this way, the British managed to influence public opinion in Indonesia without risking detection. Citing a number of news items which the Information Research Department (IRD) distributed despite knowing them to be false – including PKI plans to carve towns into districts for systematic slaughter, and a story in the *Jakarta Daily Mail* about the slashing of male genitals by female communists on 30th September. – Easter concludes that 'it is undeniable [that] Britain incited hostility to the Communists and at least implicitly encouraged the mass murder of thousands of people'.[43] Easter qualifies his judgement by noting, correctly, that the British propaganda campaign formed only a part of a wider campaign, in which the Indonesian army newspapers played the prominent role, and therefore the extent of British influence on the killings is very difficult to gauge.[44] However, Easter's observation that the Indonesian army 'did not appear to need much encouragement' should be treated with some caution. As we have seen, the Indonesian military sought – and obtained – assurances from its Western backers in early October 1965 with regard to their proposed campaign against the PKI. It seems unlikely that the Generals would have moved against the communists with such sweeping violence if they were not confident of Western support. Indonesia, a country in dire economic straits in 1965, could hardly afford to alienate both the communist world and the capitalist world and leave itself totally isolated. If they did not appear to need much encouragement in October 1965, this was most probably because, by that point, the remit of acceptable policy towards the PKI had already been firmly established by the strong ties which bound the Suharto clique to Western global ambitions, in a link that had been established with a view to facilitating precisely this sort of operation at some point. In order to fully understand the nature and extent of Western involvement in Suharto's rise to power, it is therefore necessary to look beyond the support offered in the months after 30th September – the cultivation of relations with the Indonesian Army in the 1958-65 period (described in Chapter Three, above), which included the ideological indoctrination of hundreds of Indonesian officers at US training camps, must be seen as an integral part of a wider policy whereby the United States, with Great Britain in tow, groomed the Indonesian military in order to achieve its Cold War objectives in the region.

The particulars of the British 'psychological warfare' operations remain shrouded in official secrecy. A revealing 2001 book by Roland Challis, a BBC South East Asia correspondent during this period, sheds some light on the nature of the work carried out by the Information Research Department and Norman Reddaway, who was one of the Foreign Office's most senior information and propaganda specialists. Challis's account, based on personal correspondence with both Reddaway and Andrew Gilchrist, tells of a deliberate and calculated campaign of misinformation, remarkable in its simplicity.

Since its inception in 1948, the Information Research Department's stated function was the gathering of information about communist policy, and the promotion of material for anti-communist publicity via foreign media channels.[45] Reddaway's brief in relation to Indonesia was to 'do anything you can think of' to ensure Sukarno's downfall.[46] After the 30th September mutiny, the IRD therefore focused its efforts on disseminating apparently credible documentary support for

Suharto's interpretation of to the 30th September events, with the aim of linking both Sukarno and the PKI to the bloody violence of 'Gestapu' while taking care to obscure the precise nature of the anti-communist crackdown. Over the ensuing weeks the IRD issued, from its base at the headquarters of British Far East Command in Phoenix Park, Singapore, a series of deliberately misleading background briefs for the benefit of local and international media agencies. One such briefing, entitled 'The PKI Holds its Fire', was released in December, and described a policy of mass arrests aimed at putting down a rampant communist rebellion.[47] The fact that communists were, at this point, being systematically slaughtered in their tens of thousands, was not alluded to in the briefing; the strategic defeat of the '30th September Movement' in most parts of the archipelago by this point was also suitably reversed for the purposes of propaganda.

Reddaway's 'briefings' were for the most part drawn from information received in top secret telegrams from Gilchrist himself. Reddaway received about four a week by diplomatic wire service from Jakarta, and would pass these on to his contacts at the BBC, as well as UK newspapers – *The Times*, *The Daily Telegraph*, *The Observer* and the *Daily Mail* – and international media organisations.[48] These stories would work their way back to Indonesia via ordinary domestic news outlets which relied upon the BBC and other respected international media for much of their copy. In this way, it was possible for the IRD to influence the way in which the 30th September mutiny and its aftermath were perceived by Indonesian and world public opinion, giving a seal of credibility to Suharto's interpretation of the 30th September events, while providing a duly sanitised and sympathetic account of the subsequent crackdown. So direct was Gilchrist's practically unmediated influence that Reddaway would later joke: 'It was about that time that I wondered whether this was the first time in history that an Ambassador had been able to address the people of his country of work almost at will and almost instantaneously.'[49]

On occasion, the campaign was even more direct. Under Reddaway's stewardship, the IRD produced an Indonesian-language radio programme entitled 'Voice from the Well' in reference to the well at the Halim airbase where the bodies of the murdered generals of 30th September had been thrown. This programme, made by

British agents in Singapore, safe-handed into Jakarta and transmitted from a residence close to Suharto's, comprised a barrage of purportedly nationalistic anti-Sukarno, anti-PKI propaganda. A recently declassified letter from Reddaway to Gilchrist provides a concise summary of a number of key elements of the IRD's 'psychological warfare' campaign, a list of deceptions and fabrications including: 'The story of PKI systematic preparations before the coup – the carving up of the town into districts for systematic slaughter'; 'Various sitreps [situation reports] from yourself [Gilchrist] which were put almost instantly back into Indonesia via the BBC'; and 'A flattering version of the night of the long knives'. While these fabrications helped to stoke up anti-PKI sentiments among the Indonesian public, British public opinion was similarly misled about the nature of the Suharto coup, as attested by the inclusion on Reddaway's list of a reference to the IRD's contact with a British correspondent, Gavin Young, who 'agreed to give exactly your [Gilchrist's] angle on events in his article in *The Observer* of 13th March – i.e. that this was a kid glove coup without butchery'.[50] Whilst it is difficult to quantify the impact of the IRD's 'psychological warfare' operations upon the course of events in Indonesia, it is clear that the British Foreign Office was actively involved in a deliberate campaign of misinformation, aimed at manipulating Indonesian and international public opinion in order to provide support for General Suharto's cynical seizure of power and his murderous anti-communist pogrom. Britain's role in the massacre of the PKI was certainly not central but, as David Easter points out, British policymakers certainly 'did what they could' to assist with the slaughter.[51]

Notes
1 Sukarno, *Sukarno: An Autobiography* (Hong Kong: Gunung Agung, 1966), p302.
2 Telegram (Bangkok to London) 16th June 1965, FO371/181492.
3 Telegram (Jakarta to London) 22nd June 1965, FO371/181492.
4 Foreign Office minute 5th October 1965, FO371/181456.
  5 Telegram (London to Canberra), 13th October 1965, FO371/181455.
  6 Telegram (Jakarta to London) 13th October 1965, FO371/181455.
  7 Foreign Office brief to Joint Indonesia/Malaysia department 19th October 1965, FO371/181456.

8 Foreign Office minute 21ˢᵗ October 1965, FO371/181458.
9 Foreign Office minute 4ᵗʰ November 1965, FO371/181456.
10 Telegram (Washington to London) 28ᵗʰ October 1965, FO371/181456.
11 Record of conversation (Wright/Mokoginta), 'The Aftermath of 30ᵗʰ September', FO371/181457
12 Ibid.
13 Record of conversation (Ghazali/Sukendro) 10ᵗʰ November 1965, FO371/181457.
14 Telegram (Ministry of Defence to Commonwealth Relations Office) 7ᵗʰ November 1965, FO371/181456.
15 Telegram (Jakarta to London) 10ᵗʰ November 1965, FO371/181456.
16 Telegram (Jakarta to London) 10ᵗʰ November 1965, FO371/181456.
17 Foreign Office brief 16ᵗʰ November 1965, FO371/181457.
18 Telegram (London to Washington) 16ᵗʰ November 1965, FO371/181456.
19 Record of Area Meeting 26ᵗʰ November 1965, FO371/181458.
20 Telegram (Commonwealth Relations Office to Foreign Office) 29ᵗʰ November 1965, FO371/181457.
21 Telegram (Jakarta to London) 30ᵗʰ November 1965, FO371/181457.
22 Record of Area Meeting 1ˢᵗ December 1965, FO371/181458.
23 Ibid.
24 Telegram (London to Washington) 4ᵗʰ December 1965, FO371/181457.
25 Telegram (Jakarta to Washington) 17ᵗʰ December 1965, FO371/181458.
26 Telegram (Washington to London) 4ᵗʰ January 1966, FO371/18753.
27 Foreign Office minute 7ᵗʰ January 1966, FO371/187592.
28 Telegram (The Hague to London) 6ᵗʰ January 1966, FO371/187592.
29 Foreign Office minute 7ᵗʰ January 1966, FO371/187592.
30 Foreign Office brief 14ᵗʰ January 1966, FO371/181458.
31 Foreign Office background note 2ⁿᵈ February 1966, FO371/187546.
32 Telegram (London to Kuala Lumpur) 24ᵗʰ February 1966, FO371/187546.
33 Cited in Roosa, *Pretext for Mass Murder*, p198.
34 Cited in Roosa, *Pretext for Mass Murder*, p200.
35 Foreign Office brief 4ᵗʰ March 1966, FO371/187546.
36 Telegram (Jakarta to London) 22ⁿᵈ March 1966, FO371/18753.
37 Telegram (Foreign Office to Colonial Office) 9ᵗʰ May 1966, FO371/187588.
38 Telegram (Jakarta to London) 19ᵗʰ November 1965, FO371/181455.
39 Draft brief for bilateral talks 27ᵗʰ November 1964, FO371/175250, cited in David Easter, *Britain and the Confrontation with Indonesia* (London: Tauris Academic Studies, 2004), p160.
40 Mark Curtis, *The Ambiguities of Power: British Foreign Policy since 1945* (London: Zed Books, 1995) p57, cited in John Pilger, *The New Rulers of the World* (London: Verso, 2002) p30.
41 Easter, *Britain and the Confrontation with Indonesia*, p168.
42 Foreign Office brief 25ᵗʰ November 1965, FO371/181457, cited in Easter, *Britain and the Confrontation with Indonesia*, p168.

43 Easter, *Britain and the Confrontation with Indonesia*, p169.
44 Ibid.
45 Public Record Office FO 1110, cited in Roland Challis, *Shadow of a Revolution: Indonesia and the Generals* (Phoenix Mill: Sutton Publishing, 2001), p95.
46 Churchill Archives Centre, Cambridge GILC/13/B iv. Challis, *Shadow of a Revolution*, p95.
47 Challis, *Shadow of a Revolution*, p99.
48 Ibid, p100.
49 Churchill Archives Centre, Churchill College Cambridge GILC 13K iii, cited in Challis, *Shadow of a Revolution*, pp103-104.
50 Ibid.
51 Ibid, p173.

CHAPTER FIVE

'The Greatest Prize'

Reflections on the Indonesian Killings

There is no single reliable death toll for the Indonesian mass murder of 1965-66; the withering indifference of foreign minister Adam Malik's sardonic comment – 'We'd never taken a census before the coup. We didn't take one after.'[1] – provides an instructive appraisal of the Suharto regime's position. Numerous different studies by foreign academics have arrived at widely ranging figures. There is general agreement that the lowest estimate, of 150,000 deaths (from a study by Washington-based academic Donald Kirk in 1966), is unrealistically low. There is also some degree of uncertainty at the higher end, with a number of studies arriving at a figure in the region of one million (KOPKAMTIB, the state organisation which organised the killings, claimed a death toll of one million). Nevertheless there is general agreement that the true figure is somewhat nearer to the higher figure than the lower one, and a figure somewhere around half a million is accepted as realistic by most scholars. The bulk of the killing was over by April 1966. Beyond April, some intelligence reports suggested a functioning underground communist 'counter-government' based at Blitar in East Java and supported by local Chinese. Several leading PKI members who had survived the original purges – Hutepea, Tjugito, Munir, Sukatno and Rewang – were apprehended in July 1968, and by early 1969 the PKI's capability to reorganise itself had been brought to an end.[2] In the atmosphere of fear engendered by the massacres, even left-wing members of the nationalist PNI were under threat.

The mass killings in Indonesia in 1965-66 constitute one of the largest mass murders of the modern times. Yet, as Geoffrey Robinson points out, they have received relatively little academic and popular attention, especially by comparison with the enormous attention paid to comparable state-led massacres, such as those perpetrated by Pol Pot's murderous Khmer Rouge in Cambodia in the 1970s.[3] Condemnation of the killings, in political circles and mainstream media, has been virtually non-existent or, at best, couched in a language of apologism. A CIA intelligence report of 1968 observes that the massacres 'rank as one of the worst mass murders of the twentieth century'; in geopolitical and strategic terms, as well as in absolute numerical terms, the killings were 'far more significant than many other events that have received much greater publicity'.[4] The most persuasive explanation for this discrepancy may be located in Noam Chomsky and Edward Herman's notion of the 'constructive bloodbath'.[5] During the Cold War era, a bloodbath perpetrated by states who professed a communist ideology would be treated, by Western politicians and mainstream media, with the appropriate level of humanitarian concern and moral outrage. By contrast, where mass murder was perpetrated by states whose ideological objectives accorded with US economic and strategic interests, every reasonable effort would be made, at state level, to provide political, military, economic and logistical support (along with support in the form of 'psychological warfare' operations) to support the repression; the mainstream media would, for their part, do their utmost to marginalise the discussion of these 'constructive' bloodbaths, and any discussion of the issue would be couched in apologistic terms, playing down the scale of the violence and placing a disproportionate emphasis upon mitigating circumstances. This approach has also obtained, to a lesser but nevertheless significant extent, in the academic literature.

Of the primacy of Cold War strategic considerations in dictating US policy on Indonesia there can be little doubt. As Barry Gill observes, the three major wars fought by the US during the three decades after the Second World War were all in East Asia, indicating the importance that the US attached to preserving a capitalist economic sphere in that region in order to maintain and enhance its global hegemony.[6] After the Pacific War there was, initially, no single hegemonic successor to Japan in Asia; the gradual ascendancy of US economic interests in the region resulted in a US policy of allying itself with conservative élites to preserve enclaves of capitalism in China, Korea and Indochina. The policy of the United States must be considered within this framework in order to be understood fully. The Indonesian case was an example of what contemporary policymakers called 'containment', which meant achieving the desired objective (of keeping Indonesia firmly within the capitalist sphere, on terms favourable to the US and the international financial institutions) by means of covert action and destabilisation, rather than recourse to full-scale military force on the part of the US.[7]

Suharto's Coup

The most significant immediate consequence of the events of 1965-66 was the rise to power of General Suharto, flanked by his civilian advisers, the right-wing politician Adam Malik and the Sultan of Jogjakarta, Hamengku Buwono IX. Together, these three men would dominate Indonesian politics for years to come. Adam Malik became the new regime's foreign minister, and the Sultan took responsibility for the economy on Suharto's behalf, as coordinator of economic affairs. By July 1966, the United States was engaged in discussions with technocrats to consider rescheduling Indonesia's long-standing debt burden, alongside increased commitments on short-term food aid and long-term economic and military assistance. A long-term economic recovery would assist the Suharto regime in obtaining a degree of domestic credibility and legitimacy which would form the basis of Suharto's 32-year tenure as Indonesia's head of state. The bloody violence of the 1965-66 period would come to characterise the Suharto regime, which deliberately built a state mythology around the 30th September 'coup' and its aftermath. The alleged role of the PKI in instigating the 'Gestapu' affair became 'the supreme fact of history from which the very legitimacy of the Suharto regime was derived'[8]; an imposing monument was erected at Lubang Buaya, with towering statues of the murdered generals and an elaborate mural depicting PKI atrocities and the cleansing of the nation by gallant soldiers. The new regime, which prohibited the distribution of Marxist literature and banned any public discourse about Marxism, thus defined itself almost entirely by its anti-communism – a perpetual state of emergency was constructed in order to justify the long-term suspension of any semblance of democratic party politics; in John Roosa's words, the regime 'would not allow communism to die because the regime defined itself in dialectical relation with it, or rather the simulacrum of it'.[9] This sense of crisis would help overturn the traditions of an entire generation of nationalists inspired by Sukarno's *Pancasila* ideals.[10]

Under the self-styled 'New Order', the Indonesian army dominated the government machinery at all levels. Power was nominally shared with civilians, but the latter had to fit into a system in which the military held effective power. The army achieved a strong influence over government policies, with officers – who had the ultimate power of issuing licenses and granting contracts – distributing benefits and dispensing patronage to their colleagues and friends.[11] The result was a system of cronyism that was to become notoriously corrupt. The repressive state apparatus mobilised by Suharto during his rise to power was retained and enhanced under the New Order: after the abolition of emergency regulations in 1967, local commanders carried out internal security functions as agents of Kopkamtib (Operational Command to Restore Security and Order), the organisation which had overseen the anti-PKI massacre. This became the Suharto government's main instrument of political control, suppressing civilian dissent with virtually unlimited power. Kopkamtib was later supplemented by a new intelligence service called the State Intelligence Coordinating Body (Bakin), which was particularly active in watching internal activity in political parties and the Chinese community, monitoring developments and trying, in particular, to spot any signs of a resurgence among the political left.[12]

As soon as Suharto had decommissioned Sukarno's last cabinet in the middle of March 1966, imprisoning fifteen ministers and personally appointing their replacements, at the same time appointing himself acting president (Sukarno remained the nominal head of state until the middle of 1967), the United States opened the taps of economic aid, with concessionary sales of 50,000 tons of rice in April, along with 75,000 tons of cotton. In June 1966, the new regime received $60million in emergency foreign exchange credits from Germany, Japan, Great Britain and the US.[13] The US State Department considered that Indonesia's legacy of élite corruption would facilitate outside control, based on a mixed state/private economy, guided by managed foreign aid; this would have the beneficial side-effect of dissolving the state economic sector and taming the political élite, so that the country would effectively be run under the aegis of an international consortium. Working through consortia and multilateral banks, the US would use aid as a lever and re-write Indonesia's basic economic legislation. A handful of US-trained technocrats took charge of the Indonesian economy in the remainder of 1966, and Jakarta rejoined the International Monetary Fund (IMF) and the World Bank.[14] Under the nominal stewardship of the Sultan of Jogjakarta, this 'Berkeley Mafia' (so-called on account of the fact that a number of them had studied economics at the University of California in Berkeley) implemented a drastic reform of the Indonesian economy informed principally by the free market economic principles they had absorbed during their academic training in the United States.

In November 1967, a three-day conference arranged by the Time-Life Corporation, under the auspices of a self-appointed Inter-Governmental Group on Indonesia (comprising representatives from the United States, Europe, Canada, Australia, the IMF and the World Bank) effected a complete overhaul of the Indonesian economy, dividing up the country's economy, sector by sector. Many of the biggest names in industry – including General Motors, Imperial Chemical Industries, British Leyland, Siemens, British American Tobacco, American Express – were represented at the conference. Indonesia's natural resources were divided up between a handful of large foreign multinational corporations. The Freeport Corporation won the rights to exploit the copper mountain in West Papua; a consortium of American and European companies acquired the rights to West Papuan nickel; the Alcoa Company got Indonesian bauxite; the rights to exploit the tropical forests of Sumatra, West Papua and Kalimantan were shared between a number of American, British and French companies.[15] A new investment law passed in 1967 ensured that profits would be tax free, making the country a haven for foreign investment. By 1969, US investment had risen to over £200million, and US exports to Indonesia had risen by over three times in just three years. Direct investment rose from $106million in 1966 to £1.5billion in 1976. Indonesia overtook the Philippines in terms of economic importance.[16]

At this point, tens of thousands were still held captive without trial, many of them detained until well into the 1970s. Some detainees were used as servants by local military commanders, others were exploited as forced labour, and others were transferred to penal colonies. Contemporary reports by Amnesty International describe the arbitrary detention of thousands of men, women and children, citing torture of elderly women and young girls below the age of thirteen, sexual assaults on women, and the use of extreme cruelty and torture as interrogation methods.[17] Under the Suharto regime, the modest land reforms of the early 1960s became a dead letter, with the distribution of land reverting to the grossly unequal pre-1960 position. The merciless retribution meted out to the PKI in 1965-66 acted as an adequate deterrent to any poor farmers who might have wished to organise to defend their legal rights.[18] Politically, the new system was more centralised around one man than it had been under Sukarno, who had been heavily criticised in the US for his demagogic style of government. Suharto used the army to control the state apparatus with power over the army concentrated in the hands of a small clique – where Sukarno had his opponents imprisoned, Suharto had them killed. The effect of the new economic policy was little short of disastrous for the country's poor majority: between 1969 and 1971, Indonesian per capita calorie consumption was only 83% of minimum requirements, making Indonesia the poorest nation in Southeast Asia. In 1969, 47% of the rural population lived in poverty; landlessness and concentration of ownership only increased after the anti-communist purges of 1965. The percentage of farmers owning less than half a hectare grew from 46% in 1973 to 63% in 1980. While Suharto's reforms provided the stimulus for the growth of a burgeoning middle class, who benefited from an increase in the availability of consumer goods and modern facilities, the position of Indonesia's urban labourers was worsened considerably. The destruction of the Indonesian left made the country a haven for American and European-based clothing manufacturers, who could operate with few, if any, restrictions with respect to pay and working conditions. Some well-known Western high-street brands employed thousands of Indonesians in notoriously oppressive 'sweat shop' conditions, characterised by low pay, awful working conditions and almost intolerably long hours, including the notorious 'long shift' of thirty hours without a break.[19] It was this sort of access to a large labour force stripped of its rights and prohibited from forming unions – as well as the opportunity afforded for commercial exploitation of Indonesia's natural resources – which prompted *Time* magazine to describe the 1965-66 massacres, together with Suharto's rise to power, as 'the West's best news in Asia'.[20] Meanwhile the regime, which had come to power promising to cleanse Indonesia of the massive corruption which had characterised the later years of the Sukarno era, proceeded to instil a culture of corruption that would exceed, in scale and sheer brazenness, anything attempted under Sukarno. This was the culture of the so-called 'sticky handshake', of which one Indonesian official observed: 'Illegal levies are everywhere, and almost everybody is involved'.[21] The Suharto family did particularly well, controlling thirty companies in areas such as transport, electronics and chemicals – Suharto himself achieved staggering wealth. The real 'coup' of 1965-66 was not the attempted mutiny of 30th September 1965, but the seizure of power by Suharto over the ensuing months, during which this formerly unassuming General displaced Sukarno at the head of Indonesia's state apparatus, and instituted an authoritarian dictatorship.

If the 'New Order' proclaimed by Suharto in 1966 saw itself as defined principally by its anti-communism, the subsequent history of Indonesia suggests that the brutality and violence of the regime's accession to power left a deeper mark on its character than doctrinal anti-communism alone could have managed. In John Roosa's words, 'the rise to power of the killers, of people who viewed massacres and psychological warfare operations as legitimate and normal modes of governance' forms as much a part of the tragedy of Indonesia's recent history as the killings of 1965-66.[22] Suharto's was a murderous regime above all else; its anti-communism was a secondary and – in US terms – expedient characteristic. Roosa draws a link between the 'arbitrary, unavowed, secretive exercise of state power' as exercised in 1965-66, and the brazen lawlessness of the vicious East Timor campaign of the 1970s.[23] It is perhaps not surprising that a regime which prided itself on having been founded on systematic mass murder would go on, a decade later, to perpetrate the horrors of an aggressive and completely unjustified war against the defenceless people of East Timor in 1975-79, in a brutal campaign – facilitated by US military and political support – which left 180,000 dead, many in unmarked mass graves. As Michael van Langenberg observes, the legacy of the anti-PKI campaign could also be detected in the *penembakan misterius* – 'mysterious killings' – of the 1980s, a nationwide campaign of state-sanctioned summary executions of suspected criminals and social undesirables aimed at cutting crime, which had the effect of 'demonstrating state power in the enforcement of civil order through the selective, extra-judicial use of force against a defined social group'.[24] It was the regime's fervent opposition to even the mildest progressive reform – in a country afflicted with gross income inequality and terrible poverty – that led to an increasing reliance on state repression to combat dissent, as genuine popular grievances were routinely ignored by a government too busy lining its own pockets. As Harold Crouch points out: 'Despite the government's achievement of political 'stability', it had no programme to cope with the inevitable growth of popular discontent which it faced except to rely on the instruments of repression.'[25]

The legacy of Suharto's 'New Order' politics remained long after Suharto's removal from office in 1997 – most of the champions of the anti-Suharto reform movement (most notably Megawati Soekarnoputri and Amien Rais) nurtured their political careers during the Suharto years and cling to official myths about 1965. The post-Suharto parliament has maintained laws forbidding public discourse about Marxism and the participation of former political prisoners in political parties.[26] Modern Indonesian politics therefore operates very much within a 'New Order' framework, with politics across the spectrum of legitimate Indonesian politics informed by the official state mythology. The events of 1965-66 have cast a long shadow. So when Theodore Friend attributes the lack of any serious attempts at reconciliation, of the sort witnessed in post-Pinochet Chile and post-Apartheid South Africa, to 'Cold War scorekeeping'[27] his meaning is not altogether clear; US support for Pinochet and Apartheid both featured prominently in the US global strategy during the Cold War, and the US has remained as unapologetic with regard to its support for Pinochet and Apartheid as it has been triumphal about the 'economic miracle' achieved in Southeast Asia. A more plausible explanation for the absence of any reconciliation would be based on the modern Indonesian state's cultural and political maintenance of the basic precepts which underlined the 'New Order', notwithstanding Suharto's removal from office in 1998 and his death in 2008.

As far as the US Government was concerned, the episode was lauded as a singular success, as illustrated in Ambassador Green's report of an interview with Richard Nixon in 1967: 'The Indonesian experience has been of particular interest to [Nixon] because things had gone well in Indonesia. I think he was very interested in the whole experience as pointing to the way we should handle our relationships on a wider basis in Southeast Asia generally, maybe in the world'.[28] The mood at an élite gathering at New York City's River Club in July 1966 was certainly sufficiently exuberant for the Australian Prime Minister, Howard Holt, to declare triumphantly that 'with 500,000 to one million communist sympathisers knocked off, I think it is safe to assume a reorientation has taken place'.[29]

Western Journalism and Academic Literature

In the mainstream US press, the tendency was to obscure the nature, and understate the scale, of what happened in Indonesia in the months from October 1965 to April 1966. The more honest conservative commentators did not mince their words: James Reston of the *New York Times* hailed the 'savage transformation' of Indonesia, from a country in which a communist party had a significant political foothold, into a regional bastion of anti-communism and an investors' paradise. The massacre of half a million innocent people was 'a gleam of light in Asia'.[30] In December 1965, a *New York Times* editorial praised Washington for having 'wisely stayed in the background during the recent upheavals' in Indonesia. Indeed, the word 'upheaval' features very prominently in much of the discourse on Indonesia in 1965-66 (including in the original title of John Hughes's influential book), an effective euphemism for 'mass murder' which gives a suitably abstract and obscure aspect to the developments. Misleadingly presenting the anti-communist campaign as an effort solely targeted against senior party cadres, the editorial praises the Indonesian army for having 'defused the country's political time-bomb, the powerful Indonesian Communist Party' by eliminating 'virtually all the top- and second-level leaders of the PKI'.[31] A decade later, the influential *Los Angeles Times* correspondent George McArthur told his readers that an attempted communist coup had 'failed in a national bloodbath that ended the career of President Sukarno'.[32] McArthur's omission of an agent in his sentence is instructive – where a bloodbath cannot be attributed to the official enemy, the logically untenable notion of a bloodbath without killers is invoked, and the issue is buried in what Robert Cribb describes as an 'anomalous category of 'accidental' mass death'.³³ The following year, however, McArthur would go one further. Reviewing the developments of the 1965-66 period, McArthur informed his readers that the PKI had actually carried out the massacre themselves (against themselves), claiming that 'the Indonesians broke relations [with China] in 1965, when the Mao-inspired Communist Party, now outlawed, attempted to seize power and subjected the country to a bloodbath'.³⁴ As Chomsky and Herman observe, such brazen misrepresentations are exceptions – the general rule is that the bloodbath is played down, along with the subsequent US-backed domestic repression that resulted in Suharto's regime being frequently cited by Amnesty International in connection with human rights abuses.³⁵ The description of Suharto's murderous regime as 'at heart benign' by the prestigious London-based current affairs weekly, *The Economist*³⁶, falls within this particular category of submissiveness to Cold War doctrinal exigencies.

Subsequent histories have also tended to obfuscate the reality of the systematic mass murder of the Indonesian communists. Hidden in the *Christian Science Monitor*'s soporiphic narrative lies an astonishing distortion: 'Many in the West were keen to cultivate Jakarta's new moderate leader, Suharto'.³⁷ As Chomsky points out, the word 'moderate' in that sentence must be understood with an 'appropriate casuistic interpretation'.³⁸ Chomsky and Herman identify three distinct, but inter-linked aspects to the significance of the Indonesian killings: the killings marked a new phase in counter-revolutionary violence in the Cold War era, marked by resort to mass extermination for the consolidation of political power; the episode provided a revealing demonstration of the US establishment's response to a major bloodbath in circumstances in which the political results were positive for the US; and the enthusiastic response of journalists and political leaders, combined with only minimal protest at the mass killings, set a precedent for the use of mass killings as a viable model for further large-scale anti-communist pogroms in later years.³⁹ A mere seven years would elapse before the United States sponsored a similar programme of destabilisation and killing – albeit with a death toll in the thousands rather than in the hundreds of thousands –

which brought the military dictator Augusto Pinochet to power in Chile. The Indonesian experience showed US policymakers that they could involve the US government in a policy of deliberate, politically-motivated mass murder of civilians without having to fear a substantial domestic backlash from the US political establishment or mainstream media organisations. In this way, the culture of state-sponsored terrorism which characterised the United States' conduct of international relations during the Cold War era was consolidated after the tentative steps taken in the 1950s.[40] A new set of normative assumptions about the relative value of *communist* human life was inculcated, expanding on existing prejudices based purely on racial hatred. So the respected academic Justus Van der Kroef could write solemnly of his concern that 'it is to be feared, innocent victims of mere hearsay were killed [in the anti-PKI campaign]'[41]; true communists, by implication, would have deserved their fate – summary execution, often preceded by mutilation and, if the victim was female, rape – purely on account of their political affiliation.

Theodore Friend considers the relevance of the Indonesian spiritual concept of *nrima* – the passive acceptance of one's prescribed lot in life – to the resigned air with which many victims of the killings approached their deaths.[42] A more likely – if less sensationalistic – explanation is that the victims 'were paralysed by that combination of uncertainty and vague hope which makes acquiescence right until the very last moment seem wiser than resistance'.[43] The presumption that the Indonesians' resignation, unlike that of, for example, the millions of Jews who allowed themselves to be led to their deaths with equal meekness during the Nazi holocaust, was rooted in spiritual-religious cultural precepts rather than human rationality, belongs to that same strain of Orientalist thinking that produced John Hughes's offensive notion of a 'mass joyful deathwish'. In *The Politics of Indonesia*, Damien Kingsbury devotes one solitary page to discussion of the killings ('it is difficult to adequately outline the slaughter', he explains), which he attributes to a 'blood-lusting beast' which may some day 'awaken again and consume so many so remorselessly'.[44] More generally, the propaganda of the Suharto regime has been internalised by scholarship to a quite surprising extent: academics of every persuasion almost invariably use the heavily-loaded term 'Gestapu', without inverted commas, to refer to the 30th September mutiny; the majority also describe the latter as a 'coup' without qualification.

The Left

If the biased treatment of the killings in Western political and media establishments is relatively unsurprising, the PKI's uncertain position within the world communist movement (see Chapter One) has ensured that the killings have received a similarly obscure treatment in left circles, where the killings have been presented, in Robert Cribb's words, by means of 'a vague account of white terror' rather than detailed analysis.[45]

After the killings, in November 1966, surviving PKI members in exile in China published a self-criticism entitled 'General Line of the Indonesian Revolution'. The document highlighted the fact that the class content of *Nasakom* was the 'working class, the national bourgeoisie, and even elements of the compradors, the bureaucratic-capitalists and landlords', with the effect of 'not only obscuring the class content of the national united front, but radically changing the meaning of the revolutionary national united front into an alliance of the working class with all the other classes'.[46] This analysis appears to accept as valid the criticisms levelled at the PKI prior to the 1965-66 period – that their policy of working with the bourgeois and reactionary elements of the state (Sukarno, the nationalists, and the army) represented a fundamental deviation from orthodox Marxist thinking. However, the document goes on to insist that the PKI leadership's overall success was correct, citing the electoral successes of the 1950s. In the view of the new, re-grouped PKI, it was the leadership's decision to involve itself with the 'adventurist' 30th September affair which alone represented a deviation from the correct path. The leadership had sought to remove the party's main opposition, the right-wing army leadership, to redirect Indonesia on the revolutionary road that had played such an important part in the nation's political thinking; this was an 'opportunist gamble', which failed disastrously.[47]

Many overseas communist groups had disapproved of the PKI's policy of peaceful co-operation with Sukarno's state, and felt accordingly vindicated. In a December 1966 broadcast, Radio Moscow blamed the 'Indonesian tragedy' on Chinese 'adventurism', accusing China of undermining the faith of emerging countries previously sympathetic towards communism. Expanding on this theme in a March 1967 broadcast, the Russians attacked 'the Peking dogmatists, who seek to play the national liberation movement off against other revolutionary forces', arguing that this 'resulted in Indonesia's partial departure from the progressive forces of the present and its isolation'.[48] Moscow's policy of backing bourgeois, even reactionary non-communist forces provided that they would break ties with the United States, had been justified by the Russians on essentially pragmatic grounds, and attacked as a sell-out by many in the world communist movement. In theoretical terms, the Russian argument is convincing: the PKI's success was always contingent on the support of its petty bourgeois membership; this support had proved ephemeral, as in the months after the 'coup' the petty bourgeois membership ultimately sided with the Suharto campaign, acting as a fifth column to help locate and destroy party members.[49] However, it was not mere class antagonism that killed half a million people in Indonesia in 1965-66 – it was a systemised structure of killing, backed by military might. The greater part of Indonesia's military resources had been supplied by the Soviet Union, who continued to supply arms to Indonesia even when it was abundantly clear that they were being used to massacre communists. In this context, the Soviet attempt to attribute the killings to some sort of naïve scientific miscalculation on the part of the Indonesian communists, with the Soviet Union portrayed as a disinterested onlooker, appears somewhat disingenuous, given that the Soviet Union, at this time, was part of the reactionary apparatus against whose dangers they so earnestly warned. The USSR certainly did not let Suharto's staunch anti-communism interfere with state relations – the Soviet Union agreed to reschedule Indonesia's debt payments after a visit from Adam Malik in November 1966. Nevertheless, the exiled PKI was candid in its appraisal of the party's demise: despite some proletarian participation, the Indonesian state under 'Guided Democracy' remained 'a state ruled by the bourgeoisie', so that it was 'a great mistake to assume that the existence of such a [bourgeois-dominated state] signified a fundamental change in the class character of the state power ... or of a pro-people aspect within the state power'.

The remnants of the party were now openly refuting the assertion by their late leader DN Aidit that a 'pro-people' aspect had come to dominate Sukarno's state in the mid-1960s. In failing to recognise that Sukarno's state had remained intrinsically bourgeois and reactionary, the PKI under Aidit had 'made concessions in the theoretical field, wanting to make Marxism, which is the ideology of the working class, the property of the whole nation, which includes the exploiting classes hostile to the working class'. The self-criticism attributed this policy to a 'revisionist shift' which coincided with Aidit's leadership. In attacking Aidit's 'two aspects' theory as being completely different from a 'theory of structural reform', the remnants of the PKI were essentially falling into line with the Soviet approach of seeking to achieve socialism through parliamentary means.[50] The PKI's revised stance converged with the assessment of Radio Prague that the PKI's destruction demonstrated that 'leftist extremism is an immense danger to any progressive movement', because it 'delivers its supporters to the tender mercies of the attacking enemy'.[51]

Internationally, the destruction of the PKI called into question the Chinese Communist Party's position of leadership within the radical wing of international communism, causing the communist parties of Japan and Korea to realign with the Soviet Union. The Chinese, for their part, observed in April 1966 that the convocation of a 'parliament' of Suharto appointees, alongside the maintenance of Sukarno as a figurehead, constituted an attempt to 'legalise' Suharto's coup by providing a veneer of legitimacy to what was actually a violent seizure of state power.[52] In Marxist terms, the structural framework of the 'New Order's' relationship with Western capitalism is accurately explained by Barry Gills's notion of a class alliance 'between the élite of the core and the periphery', which is struck 'in order to keep the client countries' economies open to foreign capital and to discipline the domestic work force, by increasing the rate of profit via authoritarian stability'[53]: this provides an accurate summary of the basis of General Suharto's 32-year dictatorship, and a convincing explanation of the willingness of American and British governments to support his accession to power. To its shame the left, led by the Soviet Union, has tended to dismiss the massacres as a direct consequence of the naïve folly of Aidit and the PKI – in so doing, it has accepted the notion of a basic equivalence, carefully cultivated by the Suharto regime, between the 'Gestapu' coup and the PKI as a whole, along with the notion that the party somehow brought upon itself, on account of tactical and strategic errors, the massacres of 1965-66. This approach serves to over-state the extent to which socialists and communists had autonomy and agency in a geopolitical context in which they had been identified for destruction by powerful domestic and international actors. The persistence of Suharto and Nasution, their fervently ideological outlook, and the commitment of both the US and the USSR to supporting the anti-communist military clique, strongly suggest that the violent demise of the PKI was only a question of time. The PKI's policy of land reform, and the threat it posed to US oil and rubber interests in the region, meant that its continued ascendancy in Indonesian politics was incompatible with US global strategy, and it therefore had to be removed. Had the PKI continued along the path of peaceful co-operation within 'Guided Democracy' along pre-September 1965 lines, it is likely that a CIA-sponsored Generals' coup would at some point have blocked their progress, although it is certainly arguable that, without the propaganda goldmine afforded by the 30th September mutiny, the mobilisation of civilian participation would have been marginally less effective, and the death toll accordingly lower. It is essential, therefore, that the left revise its assessment and move away from the simplistic idea of a nation spontaneously embarking on an anti-communist pogrom in response to an ill-considered power-grab: this was a systematic and deliberate campaign of extermination, the culmination of years of strategic planning by the Indonesian military and their foreign backers.

Conclusion

The overwhelming majority of the victims of the 1965-66 killings were poor, rural people who had aligned themselves with the PKI simply because it was the only political organisation which seemed at all interested in representing them, both at a grass-roots, local level, and in the arena of the high politics of Jakarta. The killings precipitated the beginning of a new era of Indonesian politics, dominated by a regime ostensibly devoted to unity, modernity and an end to lawlessness, but in fact characterised by arbitrary violence, secrecy and corruption. When General Suharto finally resigned in 1998, having acquired fabulous wealth for himself, his family and his cronies, his astonishingly corrupt tenure had left Indonesia saddled with a foreign debt estimated to be in excess of $150 billion. This debt would be paid off by IMF loans conditional upon drastic domestic budget cuts, including an end to government subsidies on oil and staple foods. The poor, again, were hit hardest. From the economic hardships of the 1950s to the present-day difficulties, the impoverished position of Indonesia's rural poor remains perhaps the only constant in over half a century since the imposition of 'Guided Democracy' in 1957.

To this day, most accounts tend to understate or obscure the nature and extent of the massacres of 1965-66; in its obituary for Suharto, the British broadsheet newspaper *The Times* makes only a fleeting reference to the killings, in which obfuscation and nonsense are substituted for plain English – Suharto did not initiate and oversee the implementation of a massacre, but merely 'unleash[ed] communal blood-letting'.[54] There is no mention of a death toll, and no mention of Western support. Although the invented term 'communal blood-letting' will have been unfamiliar to most readers, no definition is offered. A similarly apologetic article in the *Daily Telegraph* – which acknowledges a death toll in the hundreds of thousands but makes no mention of Western complicity – reminds us that 'Western revulsion at this slaughter was tempered by the reflection that Indonesia would be spared the horror of Marxist experiment'.[55] Given the inhuman horror and utter barbarism of the atrocities reviewed in Chapter Two of this study, one can only suppose that the PKI had planned a quite devastating campaign of violence upon their accession to power, in order for the killings to have been justified on this premise – there is, of course, not one shred of evidence to this effect. That this perception of the killings as a legitimate move to pre-empt a greater evil still obtains is a testament to the resilience of Cold War indoctrination among the mainstream media, almost two decades after the end of the long struggle against Soviet communism. As we have seen in Chapters Three and Four, the policymakers themselves were not nearly so deluded in their thinking. What our *Daily Telegraph* correspondent describes as 'the horror of Marxist experiment' might not necessarily entail physical violence perpetrated against the Indonesian people – the true 'horror', as the American and British officials candidly acknowledged, would be the loss of Indonesia's natural resources and workforce to the US-dominated world capitalist system. It was this 'horror' that would have to be avoided at any cost; the massacre of some half a million people was, accordingly, a price worth paying.

While Western journalists continue to conceive of the anti-communist policy, in Indonesia and elsewhere in the Cold War era, in terms that are predicated upon the protection of the Indonesian people from abuse of human rights, or infringement on civil or political rights, by a communist government, the policymakers themselves were under no illusions about the primacy of the corporate interest in exploiting Indonesia's resources; human rights, democracy and the rest could be happily done away with at a stroke, if this was perceived to be necessary to protect or extend Western (i.e. largely American and Western European) commercial and financial interests in the region. There was certainly no mention of the Indonesian people in the triumphal pronouncement of a delighted Richard Nixon in 1967 that: 'With its 100 million people and its 300-mile arc of islands containing the region's richest hoard of natural resources, Indonesia is the greatest prize of all in South East Asia.'[56] The omission of the Indonesian people – both as citizens with a right to be consulted about the government of their country, and as human beings entitled to respect for their human rights – is perhaps the most distinct characteristic of the Western discourse on the Indonesian killings. While politicians and senior policymakers have brazenly disregarded their human rights, the media (and some academics) have, by a combination of understatement, obfuscation and pseudo-scientific Orientalist nonsense (the 'blood-letting beast', the 'communal blood-letting', and so on), variously erased the victims, portrayed them as willing participants, or excused their killers, while reserving the right to raise the spectre of an ill-defined, generic Indonesian populus whose interests and rights become relevant and important only insofar as they are to be served and protected by a saviour from the 'Marxist horror' of a socio-economic system which would prejudice Western corporate interests. The memory of the hundreds of thousands killed in 1965-66 certainly deserves, at the very least, a more honest approach.

Notes
1 Cited in Hughes, *The End of Sukarno*, p193.
2 Edman, *Communism A La Aidit*, p106.
3 Robinson, *Dark Side of Paradise*, p273.
4 CIA Directorate of Intelligence, *Intelligence Report: Indonesia – 1965, the coup that backfired* (Washington DC: CIA, 1968] p71, cited in Cribb, 'Problems in the Historiography of the Killings in Indonesia', p5.
5 Noam Chomsky and Edward S Herman, *The Washington Connection and Third World Fascism: The Polical Economy of Human Rights* Vol 1 (Spokesman Books, 1979), Chapter 4.
6 Barry Gills, 'The Hegemonic Transition in East Asia: A Historical Perspective' in Stephen Gill Ed, *Gramsci, Historical Materialism and International Relations* (Cambridge: Cambridge University Press, 1993), p204.
7 Ibid, pp204-205.
8 Roosa, *Pretext for Mass Murder*, p7.
9 Ibid, p13.
10 Roosa, *Pretext for Mass Murder*, p22.
11 Crouch, *Army and Politics*, p244.
12 Ibid, pp222-223.
13 Roosa, *Pretext for Mass Murder*, p197.
14 Kolko, *Confronting the Third World*, pp183-184.
15 Pilger, *New Rulers of the World*, pp41-42.
16 Kolko, *Confronting the Third World*, p184.
17 Amnesty Internation, *Indonesia*, AI 1977, p9 and p76, cited in Chomsky and Herman, *The Washington Connection*, p209.
18 Benedict Anderson, 'Last Days of Indonesia's Suharto?' in *Southeast Asia Chronicle*, No 62, July/August 1978, p13, cited in Chomsky and Herman, *The Washington Connection*, p210.
19 Pilger, *New Rulers of the World*, p18.
20 *Time Magazine*, 15th July 1966, cited in Pilger, *New Rulers of the World*, p35.
21 Barry Newman, '"Sticky Handshakes" Are Coming Unglued A Bit in Indonesia', *Wall Street Journal* 8th December 1977, cited in Chomsky and Herman, *The Washington Connection*, p212. The term 'sticky handshake' connoted the exchange of metaphorical 'sticky' sweeteners (e.g. sugar or honey) during business transactions.
22 Roosa, *Pretext for Mass Murder*, p225.

23 Ibid, p225.
24 Michael van Langenberg, 'Gestapu and State Power in Indonesia', in Cribb, *Indonesian Killings*, pp60-61.
25 Crouch, *Army and Politics*, p351.
26 Roosa, *Pretext for Mass Murder*, p33.
27 Friend, *Indonesian Destinies*, p119.
28 Tad Szulc, *The Illusion of Peace* (New York: Viking, 1978), p16, cited in Scott, 'The United States and the Overthrow of Sukarno, 1965-67', p264.
29 *New York Times*, 6th July 1966, cited in Chomsky and Herman, *The Washington Connection*, p217.
30 James Reston, 'A Gleam of Light in Asia', *New York Times*, 19th June 1966, cited in Roosa, *Pretext for Mass Murder*, p16.
31 New York Times Editorial, 22nd December 1965, cited in Noam Chomsky, *Necessary Illusions: Thought Control in Democratic Societies* (London: Pluto Press, 1989), pp106-107.
32 McArthur, 'Indonesia Anxious to Replace Decrepit Arms', *International Herald Tribune* 5th December 1977, cited in Chomsky and Herman, *The Washington Connection*, p216.
33 Cribb, 'Problems in the Historiography of the Killings in Indonesia', p16.
34 George McArthur, 'Teng's success in South East Asia', *Los Angeles Times / Boston Globe*, 15th November 1978, cited in Chomsky and Herman, *The Washington Connection*, p216.
35 Chomsky and Herman, *The Washington Connection*, p216.
36 *Economist*, 15th August 1987, cited in Chomsky, *Necessary Illusions*, p109.
37 John Murray Brown, *Christian Science Monitor*, 6th February 1987, cited in Chomsky, *Necessary Illusions*, p108.
38 Chomsky, *Necessary Illusions*, p108.
39 Chomsky and Herman, *The Washington Connection*, p205.
40 In the 1950s, US-sponsored coups overthrew legitimate reformist governments in Iran (1953) and Guatemala (1954). The United States went on to sponsor right-wing insurgency groups in Indonesia (the 1958 PRRI uprising) and Cuba (1961). In these cases, the aim was to achieve a change of government by means of relatively moderate physical violence, a policy informed by the assumption that overt, mass violence would prove politically unviable. The reaction of the political and media establishment to the Indonesian killings of 1965-66 would appear to have dispelled that assumption.
41 Justus M Van der Kroef, 'Indonesian Communism Since the 1965 Coup', *Pacific Affairs*, Spring 1970, pp35-36, cited in Chomsky and Herman, *The Washington Connection*, p208.
42 Friend, *Indonesian Destinies*, pp120-121.
43 Cribb, 'Problems in the Historiography of the Killings in Indonesia', p35.
44 Kingsbury, *The Politics of Indonesia*, p63.
45 Cribb, 'Problems in the Historiography of the Killings in Indonesia', p6.

46 Fritjof Tichelman, *The Social Evolution of Indonesia: The Asiatic Mode of Production and its Legacy* (The Hague, 1980), p244, cited in Edman, *Communism A La Aidit*, p114.
47 Edman, *Communism A La Aidit*, p119. The 'self-criticism' appears in 'Build the PKI along the Marxist-Leninist Line to Lead the People's Democratic Revolution in Indonesia', Peking Review No. 30, 21st July 1967, pp13-22.
48 Moscow Domestic Service, 16th March 1967, cited in Simon, *Broken Triangle*, p159.
49 Simon, *Broken Triangle*, p153.
50 NCNA 7th & 8th July 1967, cited in Simon, *Broken Triangle*, pp164-166.
51 Prague Domestic Service, 9th Oct 1966, cited in Simon, *Broken Triangle*, pp163.
52 NCNA 9th & 11th April 1966, cited in Simon, *Broken Triangle*, p190.
53 Gills, 'The Hegemonic Transition in East Asia: A Historical Perspective', p205.
54 'General Suharto: Obituary', in *The Times*, 28th January 2008.
55 'General Suharto: Obituary', in *The Daily Telegraph*, 28th January 2008.
56 Richard Nixon, 'Asia after Vietnam', *Foreign Affairs* 46, No.1 (October 1967), cited in Roosa, *Pretext for Mass Murder*, p15.

Bibliography

Primary Sources

US Department of State, *Foreign Relations of the United States 1964-1968*, Volume XXVI, Indonesia; Malayis-Singapore Philippines, documents 142-164

UK Government, *FO 371* series

Howard Palfrey Jones, *Indonesia: The Possible Dream* (Singapore: AYU MAS PTE, 1977)

Marshall Green, *Indonesia: Crisis and Transformation 1965-68* (Washington: Compass Press, 1990)

Sukarno, *Sukarno: An Autobiography* (Hong Kong: Gunung Agung, 1966)

Secondary Sources

Sheldon W. Simon, *The Broken Triangle: Peking, Djakarta, and the PKI* (Baltimore: John Hopkins Press, 1969)

Robert Cribb Ed, *The Indonesian Killings of 1965-66* (Clayton: Monash University Centre for Southeast Asian Studies, 1990)

Geoffrey Robinson, *The Dark Side of Paradise: Political Violence in Bali* (New York: Cornell University Press, 1995)

Damien Kingsbury, *The Politics of Indonesia* (Oxford: Oxford University Press, 1998)

M Ricklefs, *A History of Modern Indonesia Since 1200* (Basingstoke: Palgrave, 2001TBC)

Robert Cribb and Colin Brown, *Modern Indonesia: A History Since 1945* (New York: Longman, 1995)

John Hughes, *The End of Sukarno: A Coup That Misfired: A Purge that Ran Wild* (Singapore: Archipelago Press, 2002) (first published under the title 'Indonesian Upheaval' in 1967 by David McKay Company, New York)

Theodore Friend, *Indonesian Destinies* (Massachusetts: Harvard University Press, 2003)

Gabriel Kolko, *Confronting the Third World* (New York: Pantheon, 1988)

David Easter, *Britain and the Confrontation with Indonesia* (London: Tauris Academic Studies, 2004)

John Roosa, *Pretext for Mass Murder: The September 30th Movement & Suharto's Coup D'Etat in Indonesia* (Madison: University of Wisconsin Press, 2006)
Roland Challis, *Shadow of a Revolution: Indonesia and the Generals* (Phoenix Mill: Sutton Publishing, 2001)
Peter Edman, *Communism a la Aidit: The Indonesian Communist Party Under DN Aidit, 1950-65* (Townsville: James Cook University, 1987)
Harold Crouch, *The Army and Politics in Indonesia* (Singapore: Equinox, 2007)
Gabriel Kolko, *Confronting the Third World: United States Foreign Policy 1945 – 1980* (New York: Pantheon, 1988)
Noam Chomsky and Edward S Herman, *The Washington Connection and Third World Fascism: The Polical Economy of Human Rights* Vol 1 (Spokesman Books, 1979)
Noam Chomsky, *Necessary Illusions: Thought Control in Democratic Societies* (London: Pluto Press, 1989)
John Pilger, *The New Rulers of the World* (London: Verso, 2002)
Barry Gills, 'The Hegemonic Transition in East Asia: A Historical Perspective' in Stephen Gill Ed, *Gramsci, Historical Materialism and International Relations* (Cambridge: Cambridge University Press, 1993)
Peter Dale Scott, 'The United States and the Overthrow of Sukarno, 1965-67', *Pacific Affairs*, Vol 58, No 2 (Summer, 1985), pp239-274
'General Suharto: Obituary', in *The Times*, 28th January 2008,
'General Suharto: Obituary', in *The Daily Telegraph*, 28th January 2008.

Abbreviations and Acronyms

ABRI	Angkatan Bersenjata Republik Indonesia (Armed Forces of the Republic of Indonesia)
Bakin	State Intelligence Co-ordinating Body
BTI	Barisan Tani Indonesia (Indonesian Peasants' League)
Gerwani	Gerakan Wanita Indonesia (Indonesian Women's Movement)
IRD	Information Research Department
Kopkamtib	Komando Operasi Pemulihan Keamanan dan Ketertiban (Operational Command for the Restoration of Security and Order)
Kostrad	Komando Cadangan Strategis Angkatan Darat (Army Strategic Reserve Command)
Masyumi	Majelis Syuro Muslimin Indonesia (Consultative Council of Indonesian Muslims; Islamic political party)
MPRS	Majelis Permusyawaratan Rakyat Sementara (Provisional People's Consultative Assembly)
Nekolim	Neo-colonialists and Imperialists
NU	Nahdlatul Ulama (Council of Muslim Scholars; Islamic political party)
Permesta	Perjuangan Semesta (Sulawesi-based rebel movement)
PKI	Partai Komunis Indonesia (Indonesian Communist Party)
PNI	Partai Nasional Indonesia (Indonesian Nationalist Party)
PRC	People's Republic of China
PRRI	Pemerintah Revolusioner Republik Indonesia (Revolutionary Government of the Indonesian Republic)
PSI	Partai Sosialis Indonesia (Indonesian Socialist Party)
RPKAD	Army Paracommando Regiment
SOBSI	Sentral Organisasi Buruh Seluruh Indonesia (All-Indonesia Workers' Organisation Centre)

Index

Aidit, Dipa Nusantara 27-29, 34, 36-37, 41, 44, 47, 75, 126-127
Ansor 49-53, 56, 100

BTI 22, 30, 49, 53
Borneo 94, 96, 98-99
British Broadcasting Corporation (BBC) 105, 108-109

Catholic Party 21, 23
Central Intelligence Agency (CIA) 33, 40, 76, 78, 82, 84-85, 88, 114, 127
Chinese community in Indonesia 46, 74, 78, 116
Christian Science Monitor magazine 122
Cold War 68, 75, 84, 88-89, 96, 107-108, 114, 120, 122-123, 128-129
'Confrontation' 25, 26, 94-107

Daily Telegraph newspaper 128-129
Dhani, Omar 27

East Timor 119
The Economist magazine 122
Edhie, Sarwo 44, 55-56
Eisenhower, Dwight 68
Elections 22, 24, 29

Gerwani 32, 41, 51, 55, 57
Gilchrist, Andrew 97, 101, 105, 108-110
'Guided Democracy' 23, 31, 32, 127-128
Great Britain 25, 64, 94-110, 126
Green, Marshall 62, 71, 74, 78, 80-81, 86-88, 120

Harian Rakjat newspaper 33, 72
Hughes, John 59-60, 121, 123

Indonesian army 22, 24-27, 29-37, 40, 42-48, 52-54, 56-57, 59, 61, 63-64, 69-78, 81, 83-85, 87, 95-104, 107-108, 116, 124-5, 127
Indonesian army strategic reserve (Kostrad) 33, 47, 72, 84
Indonesian national revolution 19, 21, 27, 31, 104, 124
Information Research Department (IRD) 107-110
Intergovernmental Group on Indonesia 117
International Monetary Fund 25, 88, 117, 128

Jakarta Daily Mail newspaper 107
Johnson, Lyndon 75, 80, 85
Jones, Howard 70, 71, 85

Land reform 30, 31, 48-49, 53, 63, 127
Los Angeles Times newspaper 121

Madiun uprising 27, 29, 31, 40, 49
Malaya 25, 26, 94, 96
Malaysia 25, 78, 94-96, 100, 103, 105-106
Malik, Adam 46, 81, 105, 113, 115, 125
Manipol 24
Martens, Robert 83
Marxism 28, 29, 34, 78, 115, 120, 124, 126, 128-130
Masyumi 20-22, 24, 28, 29
Muslim youth groups 41 – 42, 44, 45, 48-52, 61, 76, 87, 105

Nadlatul Ulama (NU) 22, 49, 50, 57
Nasakom 25-27, 37, 124
Nasution, Abdul Haris 22-24, 27, 32, 35, 41, 43, 44, 47, 60, 69-71, 75-76, 80, 84, 86, 89, 97-99, 105, 127
Nekolim 74

New York Times newspaper 121
Nixon, Richard 121, 129

The Observer newspaper 109, 110
Oil companies 20, 26, 76, 78
Operational Command for the Restoration of Security and Order (KOPKAMTIB) 43, 54, 113, 116
Orientalism 59-63, 123, 129

Pancasila 21, 25, 37, 115
Partai Murba 21
Partai Nasionalis Indonesia (Indonesian Nationalist Party, PNI) 20-22, 24, 29, 30, 49, 53-54, 56-57, 113
Partai Komunis Indonesia (Indonesian Communist Party, PKI) 20-24, 26-37, 40-50, 52-59, 61-63, 69-80, 82-83, 85-87, 95-110, 113, 115, 118, 121-127
Partai Sosialis Indonesia (Indonesian Socialist Party, PSI) 20, 23-24, 28
Pemuda Rakyat 32, 34, 54
People's Republic of China 26, 27, 29, 37, 44, 46, 68, 74-76, 78, 96, 99, 107, 114, 122, 124, 126
Permesta rebellion 23, 25, 69
Permina 25
Pranoto 43
Provisional People's Deliberative Assembly (MPRS) 42
'Psychological warfare' 44, 54-55, 97, 101, 107-110, 114
PRRI rebellion 24, 25, 88, 94-95

Reddaway, Norman 107-110
Regionalist movements 23, 24, 69
Religious messages 40, 58-59, 77

SOBSI 21, 30
Singapore 25, 94, 110
Sjahrir 23

Special Force section [of the Indonesian army] (RPKAD) 44, 52-53
Suara Indonesia newspaper 52-55
Subandrio 94, 96, 101
Sudisman 30, 36
Suharto 33, 35-37, 43, 47, 60, 64, 71-72, 76-77, 80-81, 84-89, 96-97, 103, 105, 108-110, 115-116, 118-120, 122, 125-128
Sukarno 19, 21, 23-27, 31, 33, 34, 36-37, 43, 47, 52-53, 70, 73-74, 79-82, 86, 94-95-98, 101, 104, 106, 108, 115-116, 118-119, 121, 124, 126
Suteja 53-54, 58

Thirtieth of September Movement 32-37, 40, 44, 46, 47, 56, 72, 74, 87, 97, 104, 109
Thirtieth of September Mutiny/'Coup attempt' 32-37, 41-43, 45, 54, 71-72, 74, 87, 96-99, 104, 106-107, 109, 115, 124, 127
Time magazine 118
The Times newspaper 128

USA 33, 36, 40, 60, 64, 68-90, 96, 101-103, 106-107, 114-120, 122-123, 125-126, 129
US economic aid to Indonesia 70, 75, 79-80, 84, 86, 115-116
US military assistance to the Indonesian army 69-70, 73, 75, 77, 79, 82, 84, 86, 89, 103, 115
USSR 25, 28, 29, 68, 76, 96, 104, 124-128
Untung 32, 72

Vietnam 68, 76, 84

Washington Post newspaper 45

Yani, Achmad 27, 32, 43, 69, 71

THE SPOKESMAN
Founded by Bertrand Russell

Unholy Land
Edited by **Ken Coates**

The Second Coming of King Herod
  Ken Coates
Ref: An Official Memo - **Alexis Lykiard**
'Exterminate all the Brutes' - **Noam Chomsky**
Israel's War against Hamas - **Avi Shlaim**
Gaza and the Law - **Richard Falk**
Steadfast before Goliath - **Mustafa Barghouti**
A letter from Hamas - **Mousa Abu Marzook**
'Not simply war criminals'
  Gerald Kaufman MP
The Gulf between Us - **Trevor Griffiths**
Covering up Torture - **Shami Chakrabarti**
  Geoff Hoon MP
At the Crossroads - **Adrian Mitchell**

£6.00   Issue 103

Unholy Land

Slump and War

Slump and War
Edited by **Ken Coates**

Meltdown Election - **Noam Chomsky**
South Ossetia - **Roy and Zhores Medvedev**
From A to X - **John Berger**
Weapons for Pensions - **Richard Minns**
The Crisis - **Oskar Lafontaine**
Edward Carpenter, Unsung Hero
  Michael Barratt Brown
Reviews
Chris Gifford - Sick Planet
John Daniels - Economics for Everyone
Stan Newens - TomDispatch
Tony Simpson - John le Carré
Henry McCubbin - Spin Europe
Peter Jackson - Wilfred Burchett

Issue 102   £6.00

Subscription to *The Spokesman* (4 issues) costs £20 (£25 ex UK)
Spokesman Books, Russell House, Nottingham, NG6 0BT, England
Tel: 0115 9708318 - Fax: 0115 9420433 - elfeuro@compuserve.com
Order online at www.spokesmanbooks.com

"I've just had a chance to read *The Spokesman*... it's really first-rate." **Noam Chomsky**